Year D

Year D

A Quadrennial Supplement to the
Revised Common Lectionary

Timothy Matthew Slemmons

 CASCADE *Books* · Eugene, Oregon

YEAR D
A Quadrennial Supplement to the Revised Common Lectionary

Cascade Books
An Imprint of Wipf and Stock Publishers
199 W. 8th Ave., Suite 3
Eugene, OR 97401

www.wipfandstock.com

ISBN 13: 978-1-61097-312-0

Cataloging-in-Publication data:

Slemmons, Timothy Matthew.

    Year D : a quadrennial supplement to the Revised Common Lectionary / Timothy Matthew Slemmons.

    xx + 148 p. ; 23 cm. —Includes bibliographical references.

    ISBN 13: 978-1-61097-312-0

1. Common lectionary (1992). 2. Lectionary preaching. I. Title.

BV4235.L43 S57 2012

Manufactured in the U.S.A.

In honor of my loving mother,

Dorothy Virginia Herrick Slemmons,
a Julliard-trained contralto
from whom I first heard sung
the gospel of salvation.

Therefore be very steadfast to observe and do all that is written in the book of the law of Moses, turning aside from it neither to the right nor to the left, so that you may not be mixed with these nations left here among you, or make mention of the names of their gods, or swear by them, or serve them, or bow yourselves down to them, but hold fast to the LORD your God, as you have done to this day. (Josh 23:6–8)

The sum of your word is truth; and every one of your righteous ordinances endures for ever. (Ps 119:160)

Then [Jesus] said to them, "Oh, how foolish you are, and how slow of heart to believe all that the prophets have declared! Was it not necessary that the Messiah should suffer these things and then enter into his glory?" Then beginning with Moses and all the prophets, he interpreted to them the things about himself in all the scriptures. (Luke 24:25–27)

Therefore we must pay greater attention to what we have heard, so that we do not drift away from it. For if the message declared through angels was valid, and every transgression or disobedience received a just penalty, how can we escape if we neglect so great a salvation? (Heb 2:1–3a)

Contents

Acknowledgments

WHEN THE GESTATION PERIOD FOR A BOOK SUCH AS THIS ONE IS UNDULY protracted, perhaps the best way to recall and give thanks for the friendly agents, and even saints, who have helped it along to maturity is to do so chronologically. Let me begin with an ahistorical exception, namely, those who provided the last piece of the puzzle: the good people at Wipf & Stock Publishers/Cascade Books, especially Charlie Collier, Editor; Christian Amondson, Assistant Managing Editor; Jacob Martin, Copy Editor, and Ian Creeger, who worked painstakingly to improve the readability, provide formatting, and enhance the presentation. It is impossible to articulate my deep appreciation for this visionary publisher, which finally opened the door to the actualization of this project.

At the far end of the chronological spectrum, I must once again thank Walter Brueggemann, whose Psalms course (January 1999) at Columbia Theological Seminary provided the Spirit with the occasion to get the wheels turning. James F. Kay, Charles L. Bartow, and Sally A. Brown offered encouraging comments on the idea that arose in my comprehensive exams at Princeton Seminary (2003), which encouragement I took to heart. The members of the First Presbyterian Church, Titusville, NJ, endured many a sermon on Year D texts, and permitted me to make good use of the study to hammer out its penultimate form (2004–2005). The series of exchanges between James C. Goodloe, IV, and Arlo D. Duba in the pages of the *Presbyterian Outlook* (2004) fueled many reflections, and, though our cordial correspondence has been limited, I have taken their comments as supportive, even as I have grown in my appreciation for their respective labors in the areas of preaching and worship in the

Reformed tradition. My colleagues in ministry among the "river church-es" in New Brunswick Presbytery (2005–2006)—Greg Faulkner, Paul LaMontagne, Ryan Balsan, and Phil Olsen—read sympathetically and made helpful comments on an early (and very different) draft. Raymond Bonwell, at Princeton Seminary, afforded me the opportunity to offer a continuing education seminar on the use of Year D, while the members of New Brunswick Presbytery and (then executive) Joyce Emery welcomed a presentation with appreciation (2007). Professor Craig Satterlee and the participants in the Theology and Worship working group at the Academy of Homiletics (2007) received my working paper with enthusiasm and even beatific warmth.

The interview process for my present position at Dubuque Seminary included a lecture on Year D (2008), which apparently did not sufficiently damage my candidacy to prevent the faculty from offering me the job. I am especially grateful to Gary Neal Hansen and David Moessner for their frequent interest and encouragement, and to Jeanne Stevenson Moessner (Perkins Seminary), whose advocacy and support have led her several "extra miles" out of her way.

My students in the Commissioned Lay Pastor (CLP), Master of Divinity, and Doctor of Ministry programs, coming to seminary with a sense of calling "for such a time as this," have repeatedly confirmed my hunches that Year D texts are, in large part and in innumerable cases, precisely what have been missing in the preaching and the practical theology of the church. ELCA pastor Sharon Baglios kindly thought through certain scheduling options with me in a helpful way (2010), and her influence will be seen in Appendix C on Scheduling Options. The users of The Year D Project website,[1] mostly unknown to me by name, are deeply appreciated nonetheless. It has been of great encouragement to watch the hits tally up since the site was launched in late 2010. That trial site must now undergo a major reconfiguration, but I am pleased that it has served its Pentecostal purpose (Joel 2:28) of providing (what my wife Victoria calls) "literary justice."

In the course of this project, some other quadrennial proposals have come to my attention. The work of A. Allan MacArthur, particularly his book *The Christian Year and Lectionary Reform* (1958), should be mentioned, along with that of the Joint Liturgical Group (JLG) in issuing

---

1. See http://theyeardproject.blogspot.com

A Four Year Lectionary (1990), which was evidently the brainchild of Donald McIlhagga of the United Reformed Church in the UK. Although I have glanced at these proposals, I have not studied them in depth or relied on them, as in each case they are self-contained and autonomous, whereas Year D is plainly supplementary to an already extant, popular, and well-established three-year tool, *The Revised Common Lectionary* (1992), which I have not sought to alter.

Since posting The Year D Project website, I also have heard from, or learned of, several pastors laboring independently at related endeavors. Steven Odom, a Disciples of Christ pastor in Murfreesboro, TN, informed me of his doctoral project at the Graduate Theological Foundation in Donaldson, IN (1994), which entailed (according to his e-mailed description) "a total re-write of the three year lectionary," to which he attached a Year D. From this description, it would appear to align more with the work of MacArthur and the JLG than with the present project. Steve kindly sent me his material while the present manuscript was nearing completion, but I confess I have resisted the temptation to peer at it until the present book flies the nest. In his Doctor of Ministry project at Columbia Theological Seminary (2009), Robert Thomas Quisenberry expands the Old Testament pairings beyond the lectionary offerings and pairs them with New Testament and Gospel texts from the *RCL*. Finally, Randall Bush, pastor of the East Liberty Presbyterian Church, was apparently well into his work on a fourth lectionary year when he discovered my work online. While I have not consulted any of the above works in preparing *Year D*, Randy's description of his undertaking suggests a (not unexpected) resemblance to my own, owing to the more limited scope of neglected New Testament, Gospel, and Psalm texts, but a greater variation when it comes to Old Testament lections, again due to the capaciousness of the "larger testament."

With respect to each of these contemporary projects, for better or for worse, I have kept my eyes on my own work. While I certainly hope and intend that *Year D* might become the basis for a variety of collaborative projects (liturgical, homiletical, theological, educational, devotional), it is important for the church to recognize that the Spirit has been at work in a variety of ways, over a long period of time, among people of diverse denominations and theological perspectives, seeding such expansive work on a number of fronts. I also wish to strongly affirm the work that the Spirit does in the prayerful quiet of the pastor's study as a corrective to the way we (especially we Presbyterians) often assume everything must be done: by committee. With the publication of *Year D*, I will feel freer to investigate and enjoy these other proposals; meanwhile, I take the knowledge of their existence as affirmation of the timeliness of, and, yes, "the need and promise" of lectionary expansion, specifically with supplementary Year D. And for this, and for my colleagues in this enterprise, I am very grateful.

Closer to home, my brother-in-law and colleague in ministry, C. Michael Kuner, first introduced me to the concept of a lectionary and has been encouraging in recent years. Another brother-in-law, Scott A. Smith, offered an open and sympathetic ear when the future of this project seemed at one of its lowest points. Grandpa John and Grandma Betty Hicks and Karen Smith graciously accorded me the use of their home in the north woods so that the manuscript could advance into its final stages. My wife, Victoria, has borne with this project, in one way or another, for most of our married life together; she has patiently endured its many setbacks with me, even as she and her prayer partners have helped intercede for its viability. I am especially thankful for her discernment and sacrifice in suggesting that I convert our week away together into my study retreat for the sake of bringing the project to completion, and I fully intend to compensate her by doing more than my share of the dog-walking upon my return.

Above all, the Spirit who breathed the Scriptures through the prophets and the apostles in the first place, and who continues to quicken this reader of the Word as he searches them daily; the Word himself who became incarnate for us and to whom the Scriptures testify; and the Father who sent the Son in love for the salvation of those who believe in him, and with him, sends the Spirit again and again, "without measure"—to the Triune God is due all thanks and praise and honor and glory for what life there is yet to be discovered in the Holy Scriptures and for whatever modest role *Year D* might play in directing the church anew to those deep sources of life. May that role be significant, and may the fruit that it bears be good, lasting, and glorious.

Introduction

THE PRESENT VOLUME HAS SEEN MANY DIFFERENT DRAFTS AND BEEN adapted to several different proposals over the last several years. Now it takes a final form far different from the original. While the missing Psalms and Johannine lections were first identified in 1999, the course of readings itself was designed in 2004–2005, the two tasks forming something of a parenthesis around my doctoral studies at Princeton Seminary. A rationale of roughly fifty pages was added in the summer of 2005, and eventually compressed into a short paper presented to the Academy of Homiletics in 2007.[2] Like many an object, however, an essay once compressed does not easily resume its former shape. Pressed into service here again, in adapted, shorter form, chapter 1 offers both a summary and an orientation to the proposal, and may be all that some readers need to read before plowing into the texts themselves. Indeed, as more than one participant stated at the aforementioned presentation to the Academy of Homiletics, the title alone sufficed. The group, not without its questions and concerns, was overwhelmingly receptive nonetheless; their collective response: "Let's get to work!"

Meanwhile, there remained certain questions to be addressed and refinements made, which I have broached from the perspective of a teacher (and perennial student) of preaching and worship. How does one teach text selection, not only its options and methods, but also its importance for the vitality and integrity of the church and its underlying theological principles: the respective roles of the Spirit, prayer, and repentance in the Christian life and preaching ministry? Chapter 2 explores many of these questions, which, in hindsight, may be a matter of whether there is an

---

2. Slemmons, "Expand the Lectionary!"

implicit and unexamined doctrine of scriptural concomitance at work in our present practices of text selection. Can we rightly assume that our favored formulaic distillations of Scripture into digestible portions contain the whole gospel and the whole counsel of God? We would be foolish to say such a thing is impossible, for "nothing will be impossible with God" (Luke 1:37; 18:27, et al.), but equally foolish and derelict in our pastoral duties to presume it is so and to allow this presumption to make us content with such condensations, abridgments, expurgations, and reductions of the *pleroma* of the written revelation.

While in chapter 1, I mention a number of historical-theological, ecclesial, and scriptural soundings that affirm the need and promise of lectionary expansion, the first two of these must finally give ground to the latter, to that which alone is the "rule of faith and life" that governs how we worship and what we preach.[3] If anyone is inclined to investigate the history of preaching and, specifically, the direct link between the rediscovery of the Scriptures (see, e.g., 2 Kings 22) and the revival of the church, I can do no better than to recommend O. C. Edwards, *The History of Preaching*, and the delightful series by Hughes Oliphant Old, *The Reading and Preaching of the Scriptures in the Worship of the Christian Church*, which recount in every age how the Word and the Spirit have breathed new life into preachers and churches that at some point appear either lost or on their last legs. Here, however, in chapter 3, it is the scriptural soundings that invite our sustained attention, and finally it is one predominant theme running through the whole canon to which I seek to raise the reader's awareness, namely, the principle that calls for attention to the entirety of the written revelation. Without wishing to imply anachronistic endorsement by subsequent councils and confessional statements, I call this "the principle of canonical comprehensiveness," owing to the sense that in each major part of the canon the reader is instructed to remember, keep, hear, do, observe, etc., *all* that the LORD has commanded, spoken, done, revealed, instructed, etc. The same admonition to attend to the totality of the revelation runs throughout the Bible, whether God is speaking through Moses or Ezekiel, Jesus or Paul. While not every text cited as an example of this comprehensive principle is included in Year D, it will hopefully become clear that this is the guiding principle

---

3. "Westminster Confession of Faith," in *BOC*, 6.002.

behind it and the one that would point the way beyond Year D and chart a course for future development.

Chapter 4 is admittedly much more than a normal chapter in length, and much less of a commentary than one might eventually hope to see. Rather, it is a crisp and expeditious tour of the composition of Year D, the contours of which were only roughly traced in chapter 1. Thus, we wend our way through the course of the year, from Advent to Christ the King, highlighting unique attributes of the selected texts and some key connections between them. For each event or season, the gospels are first discussed, followed by the epistle, the psalm(s), and the Old Testament selections, as this is generally the sequence in which the selections were made, not with any "controlling text" in view, but certainly with the gospel and the epistle lections working together to provide a sort of "front wheel drive."

Two further concerns and some future considerations bear mentioning. First, the concerns: in citing text after text in support of lectionary expansion, one quickly becomes aware of the dangers of, on the one hand, moralistic legalism (whether "to the right or to the left," i.e., in either conservative or liberal guise), and on the other, what is popularly termed "prosperity theology." While it is not my intention that Year D be used in the service of any aberrant ideology, I do hope and pray that, from a Christian perspective, the reader will (1) take seriously the ongoing relevance of the law in guiding the church's "indicative ethics" (Kierkegaard) and in chastening the covenant people when they test the boundaries of covenant itself; and (2) take with equal seriousness the genuine sense of prosperity and blessing with which God honors his people as they show covenant loyalty. The many problems with prosperity theology notwithstanding, the promises of abundant life and blessing that we find in the Scriptures and, by grace, can "already" enjoy in Christ this side of the *eschaton*, should not be disdained or dismissed for the sake of appearing wiser and more sophisticated than we are. Job is in the canon for a reason, but so too is Proverbs, and "wisdom is vindicated by all her children" (Luke 7:35).

With *Year D* finally in print, one may well ask what comes next. In the near term, the answer is: hopefully some helpful homiletical, liturgical, educational, and devotional resources. In the mid-term or longer view, if

Year D is a partial solution to a far greater problem, how shall the balance of the revelation find its way into the language, theology, and practice of the church in worship and prayer, preaching and music, evangelism and mission? How best to approach the totality of the task? Undeniably, the Old Testament remains the tougher or *larger* nut to crack. That much is clear. Perhaps it may be of service to go on record with a few suggestions.

First, while the number of years making up a lectionary cycle invites various opinions, one would think a truly biblical observation of the LORD's temporal rhythms should be shaped by the sabbatical (seven-year) cycle, something for the neglect of which Israel and Judah suffered terribly (2 Chr 36:17–21). It seems to me that James A. Sanders' vision for a complete canonical lectionary[4] could easily be fulfilled in a seven-year model, something that Scripture itself envisions, even commands (Deut 31:10–11), that is, if we may again make allowance for the great historical fluidity with which the concept of canon has been understood.

Second, with the idea of a sabbatical cycle in view, and thus four additional years (including Year D) in which to read through the Old Testament, a thoroughly canonical course could be set, especially with two guiding principles set in place: (1) the practice of selecting texts coherently and "episodically," that is, without overriding concern for the length of the lection, but allowing the preacher to narrow in on the main idea and to flesh out the context, "the rest of the story," where an Old Testament episode may span several chapters; (2) the possibility of multiple (optional) courses through major divisions of the Old Testament should be allowed. For instance, the Psalms having been thoroughly used, or nearly so, it seems to me that the concept and function of "Psalter" might be expanded to include other songs, canticles, wisdom poetry, and even prophetic oracles that take poetic form. Further, in sketching the outline of a hypothetical Year E, in which the primary "Gospel" is Acts, and the primary "Epistle" is Revelation, an oracular "Psalter" of sorts, and possibly two additional (optional) tracks through the Old Testament could be provided. The need for this double track would be mitigated if two additional years (F and G) were allowed to complete such a sabbatical cycle. This sabbatical expansion may be difficult for the reader to entertain at present, or appear unduly impractical, premature, even overwhelming.

---

4. Sanders, "Canon and Calendar," 259–63.

Before we close consideration of the topic entirely, however, let me suggest a third area for future development.

One feature of biblical temporality that neither the *RCL* nor Year D address, at least not sufficiently, is the fact that the annual and sabbatical rhythms as we find them in Scripture assign an important, even eschatological, role to the fall feasts of Judaism: Trumpets (*Rosh Hashanah*), the Day of Atonement (*Yom Kippur*), and Booths/Tabernacles (*Sukkoth*), the latter of which culminates in the Great (Eighth) Day (*Simchat Torah*), when the Torah cycle begins anew. If Year D's innovation of an extended course through the Passion spans the period in which Yom Kippur may fall, then, apart from readings of Deuteronomy 31 and Zechariah 14 during the eschatological discourse and Deuteronomy 16 at the commencement of the Passion, it does little to commemorate the historical or anticipate the future significance of the great harvest. I do think the indication by the late Thomas J. Talley of a connection between Epiphany and Tabernacles, "vague" though it might be, is promising in this regard, for it certainly has patristic roots, as Talley himself demonstrated.[5] From an Old Testament perspective, we should certainly be open to learning the lesson regarding the observance of Tabernacles that the Hebrews learned the hard way, that is, the long, circuitous, dreadful way of exile and restoration (Leviticus 23; Nehemiah 8), while from a New Testament perspec-

---

5. Talley observed that Chrysostom and other patristic writers frequently drew an analogy between the older triad of Christian festivals and the three pilgrim festivals of Judaism: Pascha and Passover, Pentecost and Weeks, Epiphany and Tabernacles. See Talley, *Origins of the Liturgical Year*, 136–37. Talley also devoted a great deal of space to the question of whether or not January 6 was the actual date of the nativity of Jesus, as Epiphanius and Ephraim the Syrian held. He was not convinced by the common view that December 25 was merely an appropriation of a pagan solstice celebration. The argument is complex, but convincing. While "it seems certain that Christmas was established before Epiphany," there is considerable evidence that Christmas/Epiphany marked the head of the liturgical year; ibid., 87. Talley further noted that, in the current *RCL*, the end of Ordinary Time shows an increasing focus on the second coming; ibid., 79–80. By this he means, e.g., the Thessalonian correspondence, Matt 22:1—23:12; 25; and Luke 19:1–10; while Advent begins with the return of Christ (First Sunday), it soon recalls the forerunner (Second and Third Sundays), then turns to the annunciation (Fourth Sunday) and nativity; in other words, there is a shift in Advent from eschatological prolepsis to historical anamnesis, from forward-looking to backward-looking. Most importantly, Talley ended his fine study with a provocative loose thread: "the gnawing persistence of hints connecting Tabernacles with Epiphany. . . . Those hints, too vague to afford even a basis for a hypothesis, suggest that the relationship of Epiphany to Tabernacles should at least be accorded a place in the unaddressed agenda of this study that may merit future attention." Ibid., 237.

tive, it appears we have for too long muted the connection between the *parousia* or second advent/epiphany and the reaping imagery in which it is frequently couched. If Talley's hunch has merit, as I think it does, then it would seem the UK's Joint Liturgical Group was onto something when they extended the beginning of the church year (the commencement of Advent) backwards into the fall season by some weeks;[6] this would be a fitting way (whether with five or more additional weeks, I will not venture here) to conclude such a sabbatical cycle, that is, in a hypothetical Year G.

And what of the New Testament? If Acts and Revelation were to occupy the better part of a fifth year and thus complete the coverage of the New Testament, my first inclination would be to arrange the Gospels consecutively and roughly in accordance with the old *Westminster Directory* (1644),[7] which called for reading one full chapter from each testament per week. At that pace, assigning Matthew and Mark to Year F would leave eight weeks when longer chapters could be subdivided, while scheduling Luke and John for Year G would provide two weeks each for seven of the longest chapters (e.g., John 6). But this is as far down the road as I am inclined to squint at this juncture. Such a sabbatical model must remain on the drawing board for now, perhaps for a whole other generation to fully design and implement, one that, by the grace of God, is hopefully capable of "greater attention" than ours.

6. Goldingay, "Canon and Lection," 89.

7. Thompson, *Liturgies of the Western Church*, 345–71; esp. 358.

Abbreviations

BO   *The Constitution of the Presbyterian Church (USA). Part II—Book of Order (2011-2013)*. Louisville: The Office of the General Assembly, 2011.

BOC   *The Constitution of the Presbyterian Church (USA). Part I—Book of Confessions*. Louisville: The Office of the General Assembly, 2004.

CD   *Church Dogmatics*. 4 vols. Karl Barth. Edited and translated by G. W. Bromiley and T. F. Torrance. Edinburgh: T. & T. Clark, 1936–58.

JLG   Joint Liturgical Group (JLG 2). *A Four Year Lectionary*. Norwich, UK: Canterbury, 1990.

RCL   The Consultation on Common Texts. *The Revised Common Lectionary*. Nashville: Abingdon, 1992.

PO   *The Presbyterian Outlook*.

—1—

Expand the Lectionary!

The Need and Promise of Supplementary Year D

INTRODUCTION

THOSE WHO PREACH, REGARDLESS OF THEIR PARTICULAR THEOLOGICAL
orientation and diverse commitments, cannot escape the first and (theologically speaking) perhaps the most important methodological step in
sermon preparation: the selection of a text (or texts). One could well
argue that to avoid this universal point of departure is to depart from
the theological matter or essence that makes preaching "*God's* human
speech"[1] and to lapse into the spheres of aesthetics, politics, science, or
(broadly speaking) some other strictly anthropological enterprise. That
preaching proceeds from an inspired, authoritative, canonical text is a
sufficiently solid foundational presupposition for our purpose here.[2]

Given that text selection is the first task of sermon preparation,
or must at least figure among the first tasks mentioned in any serious
homiletical method, we may add that the means of text selection are
likewise well known: (1) *lectio continua*, (2) *lectio selecta*, (3) a local
plan, and (4) preacher's choice.[3] These methods are not mutually ex-

---

1. I borrow this succinct formula from the title of Charles L. Bartow's practical theology of proclamation.

2. Let me ask any post-foundationalists to consider Psalm 11 as we proceed with our
discussion.

3. Long, *Witness of Preaching*, 71–73.

1

clusive. Lectionaries often make use of continuous or semi-continuous readings; preachers may often "choose" any of the other three methods on any given occasion; etc. For the current generation of homileticians and preachers, however, these four possibilities (in general, practical terms) commonly dissolve into two: *lectio continua* (often with a view to some expository form) and lectionaries,[4] the pros and cons of which have been argued, with the introduction of the *Common Lectionary* in 1983, by Horace Allen and James Sanders,[5] and more recently, in a series of exchanges between James C. Goodloe IV and Arlo Duba.[6] Apart from some observations regarding the latter discussion, I will not summarize these lively debates between those who, broadly speaking, propound the use of lectionaries with enthusiasm (Horace Allen, Arlo Duba) and those who view them more critically while advocating a greater role for continuous reading (James A. Sanders, James C. Goodloe IV). It will suffice to observe that many preachers hold strong opinions regarding the use of lectionaries. Some are adamantly opposed to them for the apparent biases with which the selections appear to have been made, while others find them useful in actually checking their own personal biases, as well as in shaping their preaching and congregational life as a whole. Still others use lectionaries more freely, as they are intended, giving them seasonal use, not only according to the liturgical seasons of the church year, but also according to the seasons of the preacher's own life and the needs of his or her congregation.

Following an overview of this proposal, which is the task of the present chapter, the aim of chapter 2 will be to go the extra mile through a gauntlet of opposing views to explore several key considerations in text selection and hopefully elucidate in chapter 3 the primary principle that should inform the future direction of lectionary design, specifically, the principle of canonical comprehensiveness. In short, with the widespread use of the *RCL*, it is necessary (1) to recognize both the utility and the limitations of the *RCL*; (2) to admit with its critics the need for

---

4. Unless otherwise specified, general references to "the lectionary" will be to the *RCL*.

5. See Sanders, "Canon and Calendar," 257–63; and Allen Jr., "Using the Consensus Lectionary," 264–68.

6. See Goodloe, "Righteous Judgment," and "Duba Overstates Benign Influence of Lectionary." See also Duba, "'Righteous Judgment' and Biblical Preaching," and "Righteous Judgment: What Does the Congregation Hear?"

transcending its evident biases and shortcomings; and (3) to tender a solution, albeit a partial one, that honors the other *texts* (!) that the *RCL* presently excludes.[7] Thus, this proposal calls for and offers a supplement to the *RCL* (and to related three-year lectionaries, for that matter) of at least one additional liturgical year: Year D. By means of such an expansion, one that advances toward a much more comprehensive and canonical approach to text selection, the primary and most valid objection to the *RCL* (as I see it) would be substantially addressed, namely, its incompleteness. Expanding the lectionary with the aim of honoring the authority of the canon yields a tool that should carry greater theological weight with its present detractors. Further, from a practical theological perspective, this outside-the-box approach to text selection—the box in this case being the current three-year structure of the *RCL*—employs the sort of figure-ground reversal that often characterizes heuristic experiences or instances of greater revelation and precipitates periods of reformation, renewal, and revitalization.

THEOLOGICAL, ECCLESIAL, AND SCRIPTURAL SOUNDINGS

One need not venture very far down this path before signs of confirmation and promise begin to emerge, signs that such a proposal would indeed put us on the right track. Others have trodden this ground before. Consider Luther's discovery of the Pauline doctrine of justification by faith; the expository preaching of the Reformers in Europe and the Awakeners in the New World; Kierkegaard's "drawing forward" the Epistle of James; Barth's engagement with Romans and his clarion "*Ad fontes!*"; and (via Kierkegaard) Bonhoeffer's distinction between cheap and costly grace and his radical appropriation of the Sermon on the Mount. Indeed, the first word in Bonhoeffer's *Discipleship* is this: "In times of church renewal holy scripture naturally becomes richer in content for us."[8] This is not only a statement of depth, but of breadth, as well. More recently, one student of church renewal has come to this terse conclusion: "coming revivals will

---

7. An early draft of the present chapter appeared in the working papers of the annual meeting of the Academy of Homiletics (2007), the theme of which meeting was "Honoring the Other."

8. Bonhoeffer, *Discipleship*, 37; on Bonhoeffer's debt to Kierkegaard, see the frequent references to Kierkegaard in the preface, and chs. 1–5; see also Slemmons, "Toward a Penitential Homiletic," 120–21 n. 5.

restore the fullness of scripture."[9] A rediscovery of Scripture is widely recognized as a common element, if not *the* primary attendant, of genuine
reformation. Reform is virtually synonymous, or at least synchronous,
with some fresh and inspired appropriation of the written revelation.
Which Scripture texts are needed at any given time or on any given occasion is, of course, the inescapable question. But if diligence is exercised in
keeping "the whole counsel (or purpose) of God" (Acts 20:27) in view, we
reduce the risk that key texts, doctrines, and practices will be neglected,
or that some vital, redemptive word will fail to resound.

My own denomination, the Presbyterian Church (USA), makes wide
programmatic use of the *RCL*. Oddly enough, however, our constitutional
Book of Order offers only faint praise for lectionaries. After assigning to
the Minister of the Word and Sacrament the responsibility for providing
readings from the "*full* range of Scripture" and the "*whole* range of the
psalms,"[10] the commendation of lectionaries in the PC(USA)'s constitution is tepid at best: "Lectionaries offered by the church ensure a broad
range of readings as well as consistency and connection with the universal Church."[11] Simply put, "broad" does not mean "full." Thus, unless the
scope of the lectionary in question conforms more closely to that of the
canon itself, it is misleading to count *scriptural comprehensiveness* among
the positive benefits of lectionary usage,[12] or to suggest that lectionaries
increase exposure to the Bible "in its fullness."[13] The well-known (Roman)
assertion in the "Constitution on the Liturgy" should be recalled: "The
treasures of the Bible are to be opened up more lavishly."[14] Now, nearly
a half century later, we would do well to respond: "Yes, and still more
lavishly!"

Scripture itself, however, offers the most emphatic and consistent
encouragement to attend to and preserve the fullness of the revelation:

9. De Arteaga, *Forgotten Power*, 262.

10. "The Teaching Elder is responsible for the selection of Scripture to be read in
all services of public worship and should exercise care so that over a period of time the
people will hear *the full message of Scripture*. It is appropriate that in the Service of the
Lord's Day there should be readings from the Old Testament and the Epistles and the
Gospels of the New Testament. The *full* range of psalms should also be used in worship."
W-2.2002, in *BO*; emphasis mine.

11. W-2.2003, in *BO*.

12. Westerfield Tucker, "Lectionary Preaching," 305–7.

13. Bower, *Handbook for the Common Lectionary*, 27.

14. Vatican Council II, "Constitution on the Liturgy," para. 51.

"Blessed is the one who reads aloud the words of the prophecy, and blessed are those who hear and who keep what is written in it; for the time is near" (Rev 1:3). In chapter 3, we will take stock of the many ways in which this fullness is indicated in Scripture so as to form a mosaic that, in its totality, approximates and approaches the canon, even if the formal classification must for now fit somewhat loosely. What we will discover is a host of familiar and unfamiliar texts that (1) promise life where the comprehensive revelation is honored: "One does not live by bread alone, but by *every* word that comes from the mouth of the LORD" (Deut 8:3; Matt 4:4; cf. Isaiah 55), or (2) conversely, warn of severe consequences for subjectively or preferentially narrowing the divine revelation and placing human restrictions (be they political, economic, social, or cultural) on which texts will be read, preached, heard, and applied in the life of the church. What the latter (negative) texts, unpleasant though they are, have to teach us is that, where certain Scriptures fall into disuse, there we should not be surprised to experience *loss* of life, health, vitality, and energy, and this in turn may explain to a considerable extent the very depletion that many denominations have experienced in the last fifty years.

Again, the principle we have in view is not merely Deuteronomistic or apocalyptic; rather, it transcends genre. In the Old Testament, the forging or fulfilling of a covenant (Exod 23:13; Josh 22:2; 1 Kgs 9:4; 2 Kgs 21:8) is often marked with reference to "all" that the LORD has said or commanded. Not surprisingly, the Torah psalms laud the perfection and the life-giving properties of the word of the LORD in its totality: "The law of the LORD is perfect, reviving the soul" (Ps 19:7); "All your commandments are enduring" (119:86; see also 119:6, 13, 128, 151, 160, 172). But the prophets and the Wisdom literature intone the same overarching theme (Ezek 3:10; 12:23; 18:19, 21; Prov 30:5).

The pastoral epistles also strike a sympathetic chord: "*All* Scripture is inspired by God and is useful for teaching, for reproof, for correction, and for training in righteousness" (2 Tim 3:16). (Further, by virtue of divine inspiration, this apostolic "all" trumps any mitigating claims we might infer from competing theories of human authorship.) Finally, the gospels resound with the same chorus (Matt 5:18; 28:10–20; Luke 24:25–27), even to the point of highlighting the anamnetic role of the Holy Spirit in apostolic ministry, including (if we may be so bold) in text selection itself: "the Advocate, the Holy Spirit, whom the Father will send in my name, will teach you *everything*, and remind you of *all* that I have said to you" (John 14:26).

Scripture not only encourages preservation of and attention to the whole witness, it also warns in the starkest possible terms of curses and calamities that will befall those who forget, dismiss, scorn, deny, diminish, or otherwise discount the revelation. This is so obvious that it scarcely bears mentioning, but for (1) the fact that the consequences of forgetting are so very dire, and (2) the fact that Scripture itself does not hesitate, in the most redundant terms, to "arouse your sincere intention by reminding you that you should remember the words spoken in the past by the holy prophets, and the commandment of the Lord and Savior spoken through your apostles" (2 Pet 3:2).

With only this nagging "reminder to remember," I will spare the reader a summary of the prophetic tradition for now. Yet, in the interest of placing this proposal within the framework of my overarching project of a penitential homiletic (i.e., one that exercises reforming influence and hence may be considered *reformata, semper reformanda*), I would mention an interesting implication of the aforementioned Goodloe-Duba debate that raises questions concerning the seriousness with which we, in actual practice, take these prophetic warnings from Scripture and apply them to our own homiletical and liturgical vocations, for it reveals the Reformed tradition's essentially penitential character, which liturgiologists such as James A. White have tended to dismiss as residual medievalism,[15] and which even deeply committed preachers in the Reformed tradition hesitate to fully own.

RIGHTEOUS JUDGMENT CALLS FOR REPENTANCE

In the final word of his (2004) exchange with Goodloe, Duba asserts his basic agreement with Goodloe that "the righteous judgment of God is upon us," yet he attributes this to "the spate of 'topical preaching' that

---

15. "Unfortunately, the Reformers themselves had been so thoroughly formed by late medieval penitential piety that they brought this attitude to their rites." White, *Introduction to Christian Worship*, 254; cf. 161, 189 et al. "Calvin is direct heir to the Fourth Lateran Council's decree in 1215 that penance was necessary to communion; he just enforced it more rigorously." White, *Brief History*, 123. It never seems to have occurred to White that the strong emphasis the Reformers placed on repentance was a fruit of their systematic study of Scripture in the original languages, and not owing to their indebtedness to the same council that first officially defined the Eucharist in terms of "transubstantiation."

dominated the church in the twentieth century," when Scripture was regarded as secondary. Indeed, Duba speaks of the topical preaching of his generation as one duly chastened. Having made this confession, he then seeks further common ground with Goodloe (and Hughes Oliphant Old) by characterizing their concerns about Advent and Lent as a critique of "the dominant penitential tone of the medieval Roman lectionary," and asserting that both the New Roman Lectionary and the *RCL* lighten and soften this tone. Without suggesting a return to a calendar stuffed with Saints' Days, the neglect of the Psalter, or the sale of indulgences, this latter bid constitutes a pretty boggy addition to the rock on which an initial agreement was forged. Does not the reality that we stand under "the righteous judgment of God" call precisely for *repentance*? It is worth remembering that the very first of Luther's ninety-five theses reads thus: "When our Lord and Master Jesus Christ said, 'Repent,' he called for the *entire life* of believers to be one of repentance."[16] How then can it be said, much less agreed upon, that repentance is *not* to influence the manner in which we go about selecting texts or stand out too much in the chosen texts themselves?

Again, Duba and Goodloe not only agree on this matter of "the righteous judgment of God" under which the PC(USA) is (and other mainline denominations are and have been) in decline, but they also agree on an "urgent need to see the Bible as a whole." Doubtless they are in earnest on both points. Therefore, let us take this a step further and suggest that the warning at the end of Revelation applies, not merely to the twenty-two chapters of the sixty-sixth book of the Bible, but to the entire canon: "I warn everyone who hears the words of the prophecy of this book: if anyone adds to them, God will add to that person the plagues described in this book; if anyone takes away from the words of the book of this prophecy, God will take away that person's share in the tree of life and in the holy city, which are described in this book" (Rev 22:18–19).

This leap toward a canonical application will appear naïve from a historical, source-critical perspective, and indeed from just about every other anthropic angle, but from the perspective of penitential faith, it proceeds directly from the double conviction on which Goodloe and Duba clearly agree, namely, that *some* word from the Bible *viewed as a whole* and related to our systematic diminution of the Word of God must offer

---

16. Luther, *Ninety-five Theses*, 489–500.

an explanation for the righteous judgment under which we now stand. To acknowledge this and then shrink from it without venturing a concrete act of "behavioral modification" is at best to abandon the hard-won common ground their exchange has revealed. But to first claim that we (preachers, in particular) stand under God's righteous judgment, and then avoid penitential themes in our selection of texts is sheer double-mindedness (Jas 1:6–7; 4:8; Ps 119:113; Matt 6:24; Luke 16:13); it exchanges dialectic for dialogue-turned-dichotomous, and drives ever deeper the wedge that would appear to separate faith from repentance, when in fact they are inseparable (Mark 1:14–15; Rom 14:23).

Eventually, Duba modifies and mitigates his claims for the lectionary, in effect conceding Goodloe's point that he has "overstated the benign effects" of the *RCL*. But, he sighs, "it is the best we have." He admits with Goodloe that preachers' motives are "never pure," and this is no less true when "the compilers of a lectionary include only some texts and exclude others."

Finally, Duba invites us to examine the *RCL* to see what people would *not* hear if they only heard *lectio continua*. "And what do they *not* hear? If they have heard the letter of Jude proclaimed, and almost two years of . . . Matthew, what is it that they have not heard? A check against the *Revised Common Lectionary* would be a good starting point for this examination." Duba assumes the *RCL* provides a check and balance against biases in one's scriptural diet. But should we not, instead, use the canon to determine what texts are missing from the lectionary, as I have done in designing Year D?

As critical as I am of an *incomplete* lectionary (though I am less invested in the pseudo-systematic idea that every passage has to be read in its proper canonical sequence), I too have found the *RCL* a helpful tool. But "the preaching of the gospel for the salvation of humankind" deserves far better than the best tools we have yet developed.[17] If the tool we have is not perfect, and if its very imperfection and partiality have placed us under the righteous judgment of God, should not our repentance take the form of seeking to improve it?

---

17. See G-1.0200, in *BO*.

FEATURES OF THE PROPOSED SUPPLEMENTARY YEAR D

All of this begs the question: What blessing (Rev 1:3) might we stand to gain if we were to take in earnest Scripture's breathtaking (unqualified!) qualifiers: "the *whole* purpose," "*every* word that proceeds," "*all* Scripture is inspired," and apply them to the false dichotomy between *lectio continua* and *lectio selecta?* The question is not hypothetical. But it is the task of chapter 4 to explore them by way of considering the composition of Year D itself. Here we will only trace the primary contours and peculiarities of Year D and indicate certain theological emphases that are bound to arise.

THE GOSPELS

Year D captures all remaining (unparalleled) Gospel texts, including the Lukan texts concerning Zechariah and the Baptizer's birth, a significant portion of the Sermon on the Mount (Matt 7:1–20), and whole chapters of John (5, 7, 8, 16) that are largely or entirely missing from the *RCL*. It provides for parallel readings to be drawn forward where a single version from the Synoptic Gospels has been predominant. Further, it provides for a thorough reading of Jesus' apocalyptic discourse, his confrontation with the authorities as a prelude to the Passion, and the Passion itself.[18]

THE EPISTLES

Year D includes all remaining epistle texts, with the exception of Acts and Revelation, since both are exceptional with regard to the category of epistle and require special consideration beyond the scope of this proposal. The epistles that are missing entirely from the *RCL* (Jude, 2 and 3 John) are included. Missing sections of the longer epistles (Romans, 1 and 2 Corinthians, Hebrews) are fleshed out in semi-continuous fashion, while the troublesome, but also instructive, household codes and absent sections

18. In "Duba Overstates Benign Influence of Lectionary," Goodloe's main objection is the subordination of canon to calendar, particularly the ways in which Advent and Lent (which "have no basis in scripture") undermine a Reformed emphasis on prevenient grace by suggesting we prepare ourselves to receive it. For Goodloe, these objections are best illustrated, and the case for *lectio continua* is best made, by the lectionary's tendency to pack the passion narratives into a single event (Passion Sunday) or week (Holy Week), so that the lengthy reading allows little opportunity for preaching and necessitates a dramatic option or passion play. By contrast, Year D provides for a *continuous* reading of the Passion over the course of ten weeks.

of the shorter epistles are drawn in, either in semi-continuous fashion, or by way of a significant allusion or theme. In Lent, various approaches to a *lectio continua* treatment of Galatians or James are provided, or alternatively, the previously omitted passages of these epistles may be read over against one another, thus providing an interesting, highly charged, yet potentially fruitful dialectic in which to consider the tensions at play in New Testament theology. (Of course, other mid-length epistles such as Ephesians, Philippians, Colossians, 1 Thessalonians, 1 or 2 Timothy, or 1 Peter, may be treated in continuous fashion here or elsewhere).

The Psalms

Some fifty psalms entirely excluded from the *RCL* are represented in Year D. However, not every verse has been (or, practically speaking, could be) included in a single supplementary year. Many of the psalms that are reinstated are considered individual psalms of lament.[19] If I rightly understand the rationale that went into the design of the *RCL*, these psalms were considered doubly unqualified. Deemed unsuitable for *corporate* worship by way of their *individual* point of view, they are also unsuitably doxological by virtue of their *plaintive* character. But this reasoning has not been consistently applied. The popular Shepherd Psalm (Psalm 23) occurs three times in the *RCL*, despite its individual voice. Psalm 73, which Walter Brueggemann considers perhaps the "most satisfying" of all the psalms, is included for the first time with Year D.[20] Another psalm that demonstrates the flimsy rationale for previously excluding the individual laments certainly speaks plaintively in the singular grammar—"I pour out my complaint before him" (142:2a)—yet it concludes with this

19. Goldingay puts the number of excluded psalms at forty and the omitted lament psalms at thirty-two. "Now these are a form of prayer which occupies about half of the Psalter, so nearly half of them never appear. In other words, the Psalter as a whole puts on to the lips of the people of God three chief ways of speaking to God (praise or worship, confession or thanksgiving, and lament or prayer) and implies by its proportioning that the last of these is particularly important. RCL ignores this datum and follows the Church's customary focus . . . on the kind of psalm with which the Church has been more comfortable, ignoring the awareness that has grown over a number of years that the Psalter knew what it was doing when it invited the people of God to spend much time expressing to God their grief, hurt, anger, pain, and loneliness, so that it can be ministered to and responded to." Goldingay, "Canon and Lection," 95.

20. Brueggemann, *Message of the Psalms*, 115–21.

promise of social restoration: "The righteous will surround me, for you will deal bountifully with me" (142:7b). Think of the joy in heaven!

Another feature of many of the psalms reclaimed in Year D is the threatening presence of so many enemies. Undeniably, enemies appear to be everywhere in the psalter. But is it not simply dishonest to "pray around" the vitriolic outbursts of the psalmist? Is it not incredible to pretend in our present milieu that "the Israel of God" (Gal 6:16) has no enemies? To perpetuate this polite naïveté is most unhelpful, and has certainly contributed to the current crisis. Neither can worship and preaching ever become truly pastoral when the individual is never addressed or permitted to give voice and vent to her deepest lamentations. To do so, however, promises the restoration of the individual to the fellowship of the righteous!

THE OLD TESTAMENT

As I understand the concern behind the primary revisions that went into the *RCL*, namely, those regarding the prophecy-fulfillment pairing of Old and New Testament texts, the concern was not that this mode of interpretation and selection is illegitimate, but that it was predominant in the Roman lectionary. The resultant revisions of the *RCL*, however, overcompensate on this score, for this typological approach has been almost completely eliminated, rather than merely offset in a balanced manner. If Years A, B, and C are modest with respect to prophecy-fulfillment, Year D maintains the ongoing relevance of this characteristic form of Christian interpretation.

Where some have lamented a narrow representation of the prophets in the *RCL*, Year D places numerous options on the table from both major and minor prophets, including significant expansions of Isaiah and Jeremiah, multiple lections from Ezekiel and Zechariah, and additional passages from Hosea, Amos, Micah, Habakkuk, and Malachi. Finally, Year D provides for the possibility of preaching *lectio continua* through the heretofore entirely excluded books of Obadiah and Nahum and the mostly excluded book of Haggai. Ten additional lections are suggested from the "former prophets" (from Joshua through the Kings corpus).

Where the wisdom tradition and The Writings are concerned (apart from the Psalter), Year D reinstates several important chapters from Job that are excluded even from the Daily Lectionary (!), namely, the speeches of Elihu (Job 32–37), which modern scholars downplay as the extraneous speech of a comical windbag, but which the Reformers rightly understood as prophecy of the highest order bearing considerable Christological import. Further, several lections are included from Ecclesiastes, Daniel, and 2 Chronicles, the prayer of national repentance from Nehemiah, a pericope from the previously unrepresented book of Ezra, and additional passages from Proverbs, Song of Songs, and Lamentations. Numerous lections have been added from the Torah, as well, several of them "hard texts," including seven from Genesis, four from Exodus, one from Leviticus, five from Numbers, and sixteen from Deuteronomy.

THE LENGTH OF TEXTS, THE MULTIPLICITY OF OPTIONS, AND THE NECESSITY FOR "PREACHER'S CHOICE"

Appendix A to this volume lists the lections that comprise Year D, while Appendix B is a Scripture index of the lections. A cursory examination of either Appendix will soon reveal some distinctions, besides the lections themselves, that set Year D apart from the *RCL*. First, many of the lections in Year D are longer, often considerably longer, than those in the *RCL*. Further, in some cases, owing to either the length of the lections or the number of optional readings suggested, the parallels are listed with the expectation that some degree of "preacher's choice" will be required.[21] This is especially the case with the Old Testament readings and the Gospel lections relating to the apocalyptic discourse, the prelude to the Passion, and the Passion itself. It is also true in the case of the psalm assigned to the First Sunday of Advent (Psalm 18). Clearly, the typical (North American) worship service of customary (one-hour) length will not be able to accommodate all four readings in their entirety, especially in light of the emphasis Year D places on the "fullness" of the Word. Where the three-year, ABC cycle errs on the side of shortened readings, leaving it up to the preacher to expand them if needed, Year D "errs" in the opposite direction to ensure that these texts are, at very least, placed on the preacher's desk for consideration. Thus, the likelihood is greater that some further degree of "preacher's choice" will need to be exercised in order to reduce the size of the reading or take a "selected verses" approach, while ensuring that coherence and meaning are not lost in the process.

21. Where the Gospels are concerned, the aim is not harmonization, but comprehensiveness.

What about Scheduling and Ecclesial Unity?

It is often claimed that lectionary preaching enhances ecumenical unity, as it allows for greater cooperation in programmatic endeavors and liturgical planning. While this is no doubt true to an extent, one would be hard-pressed to argue that unity in the body of Christ begins and ends with everyone reading the same texts at the same time. Certainly, such synchronicity can foster many remarkable connections within the body of Christ, but just as surely the unity for which Jesus prays (John 17:11–23) runs much deeper than that. Thus, the truly united *ecclesia* can and should be able to live in and with the tensions at work *within* the canon, the *whole* canon, as well as within the church, the whole church.

In fact, because the lectionary (the "temporale") as a calendar of readings is essentially a (temporal) schedule of readings, the nature of the unity that *lectio selecta* provides is primarily *rhythmic*. In other words, the unity that a common lectionary provides is more of a metronome than a tuning fork. To employ an esthetic analogy, the four lections of the lectionary may be likened to a four-part choral arrangement and the common timing to the tempo of the piece. So, for instance, as lectionary preachers gravitate toward the gospel readings on Resurrection morning, four-part harmony gives way to unison. All the while, of course, the tempo remains the same.

To stay with the musical analogy, there is another way of maintaining tempo, yet providing for temporal diversity. It is called a *cross-rhythm*. The cross-rhythm maintains tempo, while using two different time signatures in parallel. A simple cross-rhythm might consist of a 3/4 and a 4/4 (or common time) sequence running simultaneously, so that four measures of 3/4 and three measures of 4/4 bring the two parts back to the same starting point after twelve beats.

To return to the effect that a supplementary Year D will have on the ecumenical unity shared by the lectionary-based churches, one can easily imagine some congregations using it and others opting out, for whatever reason. The effect of this dissent or departure, however, lends a whole new creative aspect, with some congregations taking up a four-year cycle while others continue to "waltz." This is not to suggest that some *must* opt out and continue to operate with a diminished canon. It is simply to recognize that not all will elect to depart from the three-year cycle, and this decision, voluntarily or otherwise, can and will form an integral part of a more complex and interesting arrangement. For further consideration of the scheduling options with which a supplementary year presents us, see Appendix C.

OTHER THEOLOGICAL EMPHASES

THE SINGULARITY OF THE GOSPEL

This musical analogy (the cross-rhythm) obviously concerns more of a formal unity, rather than a substantive or spiritual one. One of the common assertions one will discover, if one pays careful attention to the texts in Year D, is that true ecclesial unity derives from the singularity of the gospel, which in turn derives from the "uniquely unique" God-man, Jesus Christ.[22] There is no other gospel (Gal 1:6–9; 1 Tim 1:1–11), and there is no other Jesus (2 Cor 11:1–6). Even if we have difficulty articulating the singular gospel in a terse formula or creed, even if we find this gospel boiled down with some variations in Scripture, even if we have the apostle occasionally calling it "my" gospel (Rom 2:15–17; 16:25–27; 2 Tim 2:8–9), none of this should obscure the fact that the Bible repudiates the idea of multiple competing or conflicting "gospels." This is why an essential pedagogical exercise, not only for beginning preachers but for veterans too, is to practice articulating the one gospel *in nucé*, and to test this understanding rigorously and repeatedly against the whole canon of Scripture. In short, although it may be in reality too much to expect of the temporal church, with its denominations and divisions, to agree on a common articulation of the gospel outside of Scripture (though some would suggest The Apostles' Creed seems to come as close as anything), what one will see in the Year D lections is that, undeniably, there is but one gospel that corresponds to the person and work of Christ with his two natures, and that assertion alone is the sound and solid point on which to ground our ecclesial unity. A closely related point, namely, the need for and the inescapably selective character of recapitulation, will be explored in chapter 2.

---

22. I employed this intentional tautology in "Toward a Penitential Homiletic" in order to set the uniqueness of the divine-human person, Jesus Christ, qualitatively apart from the uniqueness to which each individual creature may lay claim.

APOCALYPTIC

One of the problems with the approach taken to the Bible's apocalyptic literature in the current design of the *RCL* is that it relies overmuch on the Sacrament of the Lord's Supper to bear almost the entire weight of eschatological proclamation. Although a small section of Jesus' apocalyptic discourse occurs in the *RCL* during Advent, the exclusion of the bulk of it suggests skepticism on the part of the designers of the *RCL* or at least a distrust of preachers to be able to preach from this discourse honestly and responsibly. Either way, the decision to bracket it has only sent those who wish to understand apocalyptic texts out into the broader marketplace. To risk another generalization, eschatological preaching in the mainline theological tradition more often consists of stating what the church's apocalyptic literature does not mean (e.g., ridiculing "the rapture" as escapist theology, denouncing "Christian Zionism," etc.) than of venturing constructive interpretations of what it actually does mean, specifically, interpretations that do not sheathe the sword of the Spirit and rob it of its provocative vitality and prophetic poignancy. As a counterweight to this state of affairs, Year D provides for preaching the apocalyptic sayings of Jesus, as guided by the structure of "the apocalyptic discourse" (Matthew 24) and "the little apocalypse" (Mark 13).

THE OFFENSE

Without actually aiming to offend the listener—woe to that one who *causes* anyone to stumble!—preaching must recognize that every inclination or attempt to make the gospel *in*offensive risks abandoning the gospel itself, if not by cramming it into Holy Week, then by removing altogether the potential offense: the God-man and the cross (Gal 5:11). Year D is an opportunity to reexamine the timid assumption that the gospel cannot be the gospel if someone takes offense at it or finds it scandalous. On the other hand, that Jesus himself *is* the stumbling stone may well inspire preachers to reclaim a working sense of paradox and providence (Rom 9:32–33; 2 Pet 1:10; cf. 1 Pet 2:7–8), a greater sense of humility, and a clearer Christocentric focus.

The Question of Authority and Jesus' Confrontation with the Religious Authorities

One feature of the *RCL* is that the revisers did little to critique or amend the Roman lectionary's tendency to skirt those unpleasant episodes in which the religious authorities are rebuked and exposed as hypocrites. The latent authoritarianism evident in the Roman *Lectionary for Mass* continues to undermine the credibility of the *RCL*, which (by this pattern of avoidance) seems to suggest the hypocrisy of the scribes, Pharisees, and Sadducees was merely a first-century phenomenon. In other respects, however, the *RCL* signals a clear distrust of the preacher's authority when it puts certain texts beyond the reach of the regular preaching cycle. This highly ambivalent attitude toward authority is long overdue for serious scrutiny. The church desperately needs to understand aright and model for the culture the proper use of authority, even as it repents of and accounts for past abuses.

Repentance

As mentioned above, the conclusion reached in the Goodloe-Duba debate over lectionaries, namely, that "a penitential tone" is to be avoided, is incongruous with the consensus that we stand under the righteous judgment of God. Again, given the status quo, it would seem that repentance is precisely what is needed, and the lections in Year D do not shrink from applying the needed pressure in this regard. This is not to suggest that Year D will return us to some sort of medieval legalism. Neither is the structure of Year D with its peculiar choice of texts meant to obscure or lose sight of the grace of the gospel. On the contrary, "the truth will make you free" (John 8:32)! What many of these forgotten texts do again and again is supply the referent, the theological and anthropological crisis, in relation to which the gospel may be truly heard as genuinely *good* news.

The Passion of Our Lord Jesus Christ

Perhaps the most challenging feature of Year D for both the preacher and the listening congregation, but also the one most promising for the potential revitalization of the lectionary-based church and denomination, is that it provides for not merely reading, but preaching through the passion narratives over the course of ten weeks, following a four-week "prelude to the passion." This cycle is arranged so as to synchronize the accounts of the Last Supper with World Communion Sunday and culminate in Christ the King Sunday. The intention is neither to replace nor to duplicate the Lenten season, nor to give this cycle any sort of preparatory emphasis. There is nothing preparatory about the Passion. It *is* the gospel! As Martin Kahler famously stated, the gospels themselves are "passion narratives with extended introductions."[23] Yet, the *RCL* presently provides few opportunities for actually preaching on the Passion—no, *on the gospel!* (per Kahler)—even during Lent and Holy Week. Thus, where the *RCL* places the passion narratives in the position of being an intrusion into the *temporale*, Year D reasserts that these narratives are not only an integral part of the gospel, they constitute its very essence, and as such they warrant sustained proclamation.[24]

The Household Codes

Year D also reinstates the household codes (Eph 5:21—6:9; Col 3:18—4:1; 1 Tim 2:8—3:13; Titus 2:1–10; 1 Pet 2:13—3:7) regarding which the *RCL* is so reticent. The consensus in many quarters is that contextual distance has rendered these texts quaint, if not entirely obsolete. At the risk of reopening tough social, economic, and gender-related questions, Year D includes these texts for the guidance they continue to offer and the challenge they continue to pose in times when many households languish under diverse and often overbearing social, financial, vocational, and other pressures.

Lectio Dialectica

Finally, Year D provides alternative courses for preaching either *lectio continua* during the Sundays of Lent, either through Galatians or James, or through a juxtaposition of texts, a juxtaposition that I have termed *lectio dialectica*,[25] consisting of contrasting passages (all excluded from the

23. Kahler, *So-Called Historical Jesus*, 80 n. 11.

24. The so-called Gospel of Thomas, for instance, demonstrates its unsuitability for consideration as canonical literature at first blush, namely, in its lack of a passion narrative: no Passion means no Gospel, and thus no admission to the New Testament canon.

25. *Lectio dialectica* is a neologism (irritating as such things often are), one that I have given not only to this specific proposal for preaching contrasting lections in Lent, but also to the general proposal for admitting marginalized and missing texts (Year D) to the conversation presently dominated by the *RCL* after a significant pattern of neglect, as well as to the underlying conviction on which this proposal is based, namely, that the

RCL, most likely for their problematic nature)—passages that, arranged thus, are bound to demand the most lively and considered engagement of, and perhaps exert a sort of defibrillating effect upon, the preacher, the attentive congregation, and the church at large.

CONCLUSION: "LET THE WORD DO ITS WORK!"

Nearly twenty years ago, I learned the commonplace that each of us tends to operate with his or her own "canon within the canon." It is true of the church's divergent factions, advocacy groups, and political constituencies as well. It is nearly ten years since, swooning with the realization that a full third of the psalms are missing from the *RCL*, I distributed what I called "The Psalter of the Disappeared" to my fellow students in Walter Brueggemann's winter term course on the prayer-book of the Bible. Disseminated in a bolt of extracurricular zeal (and with a kindly nod from the head of the class), the list of missing psalms was gladly received by every pastor in the room. Since then, my conviction that the church needs the Bible's neglected texts to function anew has only deepened and intensified.

But how can this happen on a sufficiently broad scale to begin to effect repentance, healing, restoration, and growth in the church at large? Here is how: *expand the lectionary!* Having yet to encounter a single compelling reason not to put these texts back in wide circulation, it seems to me seriously negligent to fail to do so. Better by far to let them speak as the Spirit would have them speak, for I earnestly hope the reader will not presume to know, at this point, how I think they should be preached. The composition of Year D is not in any way a program that will yield predetermined outcomes. It is, on the contrary, a wager on preaching itself, from prayerful selection, through honest exegesis, through humble conviction, through theological insight, to the delivery of a sermon that can effect deliverance, liberation, reconciliation, and reform. The fractious state of the church under "the righteous judgment of God" is such that no human wisdom, no political solution, no merely sociological salve will do. What is needed today is for the Word itself, a fresh appropriation

---

full breadth of the canon should be engaged, while honoring the canonical authority and revelatory potential of these texts. This does not mean, of course, indiscriminately wrenching lections out of their literary and historical settings, or preaching the speeches of specious spirits and persons, but it does mean honoring the total revelation in which these voices too play an important, if negative and precautionary, role.

of which is tendered in Year D in the most concrete, practical terms, to exercise its, nay, *the LORD's* own influence. It is time to follow Luther's reforming principle of preaching as stated upon his return to Wittenberg from protective custody on the Wartburg, an interim he spent (by the way) in translating the *entire* Greek testament: "I did nothing; I let the Word do its work."[26]

---

26. Meuser, *Luther the Preacher*, 66.

—2—

Beyond the Dichotomy of Lectio Continua *and* Lectio Selecta

I SUGGESTED IN CHAPTER 1 THAT THE FOUR MODES OF TEXT SELECTION mentioned by Thomas Long (*lectio continua*, lectionaries, preacher's choice, and local plans) generally boil down to two (*lectio continua* and lectionaries).[1] Karl Barth, for example, advised his students to stick with either *lectio continua* or *lectio selecta* so as to prevent too much subjectivity on the part of the preacher, especially where the temptation to engage in topical or thematic preaching is concerned.[2]

Barth rightly saw the task of text selection as an occasion for obedience, but obedience to whom? Although he was ambiguous as to *how* the text itself becomes master over text selection, he nevertheless emphasized that the preacher should not presume absolute "freedom or control" in this regard, and "must not act authoritatively or arbitrarily in the selection."[3] Barth cautioned against selecting texts that (1) are too short, thus allowing too much room for the preacher's thought to intrude; (2) are easily and often quoted out of context, and thereby perpetuate misunderstanding; (3) might tempt the preacher to allegorize; and (4) may be forced

---

1. Ronald J. Allen, for his part, reduces the options to three by collapsing Long's local plan and preacher's choice into a single discretionary model, but Allen offers an impressive list of the pros and cons of both lectionaries and continuous reading. See Allen, *Interpreting the Gospel,* 106–9.

2. Barth, *Homiletics,* 93–96.

3. Ibid., 93.

into the service of a special occasion.[4] Rather, Barth recommended either preaching from a lectionary, thus taking direction from "mother church," or preaching consecutively through various books. Both methods help prevent too much self-involvement in the selection process. Preachers may select texts that seem to speak directly to the occasional service, yet they must use caution when doing so in order to ensure that the text "always stands above the theme of the day."[5]

Several questions could be posed to Barth. For instance, *why should common misuse and misinterpretation of certain texts not be corrected by preaching on those very texts?* In fact, an examination of Barth's own sermons suggests they can and should be corrected, for the opening gambit in many of Barth's sermons amounts to not an analogous introduction (Barth, as is well known, was no fan of sermon introductions),[6] but a direct attack on common worldly wisdom and erroneous presuppositions.[7] Thus, this is not a question we need to pursue here.

More germane to this project, we must consider two questions. First, *what alternatives do we have when "mother church" adopts a lectionary that itself demonstrates transparently self-involved biases and themes?* Are such biases necessarily legitimized by virtue of a corporate (as opposed to individualistic) selection process and a sense of ecumenical uniformity? Barth's either/or with respect to lectionaries or continuous reading is generally sound, but he himself would be the first to concede that the church can drift into all manner of heterodoxy (hence, his own dogmatic vocation) when it privileges too narrow a selection of texts. How quickly we forget the distinguishing mark of the sect and cult: the fixation on a few favorite texts to the exclusion of others! On the other hand, as those who raise concerns with regard to preaching *lectio continua* often observe, there is a risk of privileging a certain part of the canon when the congregation's attention is focused for a sustained period on one part, genre, book, or perspective.

Second, *what guidelines does Scripture itself give us for governing text selection?* Are there indicators, instructions, or examples in the Bible itself that inform this most basic step in sermon preparation? Indeed, there are!

4. Ibid., 93–94.

5. Ibid., 93.

6. See ibid., 121–25; and Slemmons, *Groans of the Spirit*, 13, 18–20, 25–26, 43–44.

7. Barth's sermons, "The Beginning of Wisdom," in *Deliverance to the Captives*, 126–35; and "Call Me," in *Call for God*, 29–37, are typical in this approach.

WHAT ALTERNATIVES DO WE HAVE?

The tension between *lectio continua* and *lectio selecta* is not necessarily dichotomous. But when the alternatives tend in this direction, a resolution should be sought *beyond* the dichotomy at the common point of vulnerability. In each case, the failing of *lectio continua* and *lectio selecta* is precisely their evident and inevitable risk of partiality and bias, or the incompleteness of their field of vision. Yet this very "partiality"—the word applies in more than one sense!—only exacerbates the dichotomy. Unfortunately, dichotomies as such resist resolution. Thus, the needed resolution must not only complete what is lacking and correct the reduced vision, but it also requires an actual exercise of the will, a "resolve" on the part of the preacher to transcend the impasse. In the present case, the key to resolution lies in the discretionary territory that both Long and Allen, among others, only mention in passing. Year D is a *local plan* disciplined by the objective standard of the canon, yet it also provides, by way of longer lections and more options, a greater degree of *preacher's choice*, perhaps especially when it comes to the Old Testament lections.

SCRIPTURE INTERPRETING SCRIPTURE

One simple approach that can, of course, mitigate the faults of both *lectio continua* and *lectio selecta* is simply and faithfully to employ the principle of using Scripture to interpret Scripture. Texts from outside the lectionary, or outside the book being read and preached in continuous exposition, can and should be brought in to every sermon to offer a needed corrective, a fresh perspective, or a view to the whole. If the preacher does well the work of historical, literary, and theological contextualization—that is, with a comprehensive view to what is indicated by such various terms as progressive revelation, *Heilsgeschichte* (salvation history), God's plan for redemption and restoration of all things, or simply the *missio Dei*—then either *lectio continua* or *lectio selecta* may indeed be used with relative faithfulness on a local basis. What will not occur, however, is the greater resolution that is needed by the broader church, one that will advance the body of Christ beyond "partiality" and "partisanship."

CAN WE NOT JUST GO DEEPER WITH OUR FAVORED TEXTS?

A similar case could be made for simply deepening our engagement with whatever text lies at hand, whether it is chosen by sequential or selective means. As Paul Wilson boldly claims: "*Any biblical text can speak to any contemporary situation.*" Wilson admits this claim may seem "ludicrous," but he offers it as something of an article of faith based on the agency of the presence of Christ in preaching. "Because God's Word is a living Word and speaks through every text, we are safe in assuming that when we bring an exegeted text into relationship with our situation, sparks are going to happen."[8]

Wilson rightly advises that the "*choice of one primary text is helpful.*" "Imagination flourishes best if the biblical channel is not being continually switched from one station to the next."[9] He adds, "*The spark . . . we seek is not between biblical texts, it is between the biblical text and our situation.*"[10] This means that those who are schooled in literary criticism with its penchant to juxtaposition between texts "may need to be intentional in re-routing their energies," for such intertextual sparks are generally going off only on the two-dimensional literary surface. "For homiletical purposes our primary concentration needs simply to be on fully uncovering the light of one text for the darkness of today."[11]

This brings to mind Walter Brueggemann's exegetical advice to seminary students in his aerodynamic approach whereby the exegete, at least to begin with, imagines that the text under consideration contains all that we know, or can know, of God. Although we will eventually move to the consideration of the broader literary context and the function of the text within the canon, etc., Brueggemann wants to makes sure we do not shift our focus too quickly from the text at hand.[12]

---

8. Wilson, *Imagination of the Heart*, 54–55.

9. Ibid., 56.

10. Ibid., 57.

11. Ibid., 58.

12. Brueggemann, *Word Militant*, 74–83, esp. 77–78. When I offer Brueggemann's advice to preaching students, I remind them that this is not actually all that farfetched where the persecuted church is concerned, where Christian Scriptures are prohibited, where translations into the languages of (until recently) unreached peoples are rare; for in fact, as the gospel makes its way into a new culture, it is quite common for the Scriptures to make their way to hungry people one book at a time, or even by way of

In short, though neither author's remarks are offered with the specific choice of lectionary preaching versus *lectio continua* in mind, both Brueggemann and Wilson are calling for substantive depth in our exegesis, a verticality that may yet be possible even in an age of Attention Deficit Disorder.[13] As I have already repeatedly indicated, Year D is a serious prescription for "greater attention to what we have heard" (Heb 2:1–4).

Once again, Kierkegaard is a prime example of how the exegete may indeed return again and again to the same passages for seemingly endless inspiration, specifically in his numerous discourses on three primary texts: the lily and the bird versus the cares of the pagans (Matt 6:24–34), love that covers a multitude of sins (1 Pet 4:8), and "every good and perfect gift" (Jas 1:17). Would that every lectionary preacher today were able to pay such attention to the text at hand as to reach similar depths of insight and heights of edifying expression! Thus, we should not assume that by simply adding to our repertoire of preaching texts we will strike oil.

In short, I agree with Wilson *in principle* that any biblical text can speak to any modern situation, provided the preacher practices due diligence in terms of theological recapitulation and canonical contextualization. This line of thought admittedly does not advance the cause of expanding the lectionary, for the same argument may be applied to those biblical texts included in the lectionary as to those that are excluded.

But neither does the argument for deeper exegesis serve to supply all that is needed when certain scriptural wisdom and insight is simply not to be found in a given text at any level. In fact, Brueggemann's exegetical approach *does* finally allow the interpreter to venture abroad in the canon, to engage in intertextual—and, I would add, intra-canonical[14]—word study that takes stock of many uses and meanings that develop among a network of texts, so as to both broaden and sharpen our understanding of the "freight carried by particular words."[15]

Bibles, books, and devotionals that are dismantled and circulated among a Christian community that is often "underground."

13. Ibid., 4–5.

14. See Slemmons, "*Synkrinesis* as Following in Faith."

15. Brueggemann, *Word Militant*, 77.

THE CONCENTRIC RELATION BETWEEN LECTIONARY AND CANON

As essential as it is to use the Word as its own primary interpretive reference and to seek ever greater depths of exegetical insight, neither of these emphases substitutes for a disciplined, systematic, and comprehensive consideration of the whole of divine revelation. This fact is borne out repeatedly when we consider the nature of lectionaries and their reductionistic relationship to the canon of Scripture.

The word *lectionary*, we recall, has two primary meanings. "In the wider sense it denotes an ordered system of selected readings ('pericopes') appointed for liturgical use on specific occasions in the church year, thus presupposing a calendar, while in the narrower sense it is used to designate a [manuscript] (especially in Greek) with pericopes thus used written out in full."[16] Of these two types, it is the "table of readings," not merely the narrower sense of the misleadingly designated "full-text edition," that concerns us.[17]

Clearly this narrower sense, that is, a book or manuscript containing the actual readings, is what Old Testament scholar John Goldingay has in mind when he makes the surprising statement, "Scripture and lectionary form overlapping, but not concentric circles." Goldingay is making the general historical point that all the words used in Christian worship have not been and are not simply taken right off the pages of Scripture, and further, not "everything that came to be scripture was used in worship."[18] Although Goldingay appears to conflate lectionary manuscripts with service books (e.g., breviaries) that contain both Scripture readings and other liturgical elements and rubrics, the point to bear in mind is that scriptural readings contained in or prescribed by lectionaries *do* in fact constitute a smaller and concentric circle within the larger canon of Scripture. To suggest otherwise only confuses the issue at hand. In other words, any lectionary that fails to include every text from the full canon of Scripture entails a condensation, expurgation, or abridgement of the written Word of God; and this, as we have already noted and shall see again,

16. Fuller, "Lectionary," 297–99. Fuller's article offers a concise account of the history of lectionary use in the Christian era. For a helpful introduction to lectionary use (in its present state) in relation to the Christian year, see Stookey, "Lectionary and the Christian Year," 321–25; see also Stookey, *Calendar,* and Webber, *Ancient-Future Time.*

17. Consultation on Common Texts, *RCL,* 9.

18. Goldingay, "Canon and Lection," 85–97.

entails a loss of vitality in the church and a compromise in the integrity of her testimony.[19]

Nevertheless, Goldingay rightly concludes his evaluation of the *RCL* by stating: "the lectionary for the principal service each Sunday should seek to reflect scripture as a whole. RCL does not attempt to do so." In fact, the lack of any such effort is so stark that Goldingay declares, "The supporters of RCL would hardly believe that this was or should be one of their major intents."[20]

THE TRUE AIM OF THE LECTIONARY

What, then, *is* the major intent of the lectionary, according to its supporters? As far as the *Common Lectionary* (1983) was concerned, its "organizing" and "determinative" principle is its "communal ecclesiology," and in this respect the *RCL* (1992) does not depart from its predecessor in any significant way. According to J. Irwin Trotter, "Here is the clue to the fundamental organizing principle of the Lectionary: the central importance of the Eucharist in the worship of the church. Salvation is not something that happens individually, but is incorporated into the whole. Preaching

---

19. Meanwhile, we should mention a third, more modern, practical manifestation of the lectionary that occurs in the arena of printed bulletin services and inserts. In a sermon on Romans 9–11 titled "The Better Bet," Fleming Rutledge calls attention to the fact that the Epistle text for the day has been printed in the bulletin, evidently by a denominational subscription-based bulletin service, with no indication of the editorial deletions: "Look at your printed insert. You can't even tell that fourteen verses have been omitted. They haven't even put in any of those little dots. You would think that the passage went directly from [Chapter 11] verse 15 to verse 29. This is one of the many reasons that every Christian should have and read his or her own Bible. In the omitted section, Paul declares that unbelief has a purpose, and the purpose is the revelation of God's salvation to the Gentiles, who were previously thought to be without hope." After pasting together and giving utterance to the omitted verses, Rutledge goes on to proclaim: "This astonishing passage should take our breath away. The apostle Paul and the prophet Isaiah have the most 'inclusive' visions in all the Bible, yet the Bible story books don't know what to do with them. The sum total of most people's knowledge of Isaiah and Paul is that Paul saw something on the road to Damascus and that Isaiah wrote Handel's *Messiah*. We are for the most part entirely ignorant of the radical visions of these two towering servants of God. I'm not even convinced that the learned designers of the lectionary quite get it, because they unaccountably omit the phrase that Paul uses to describe God's plan for the Jews: *full inclusion.*" Rutledge, *Not Ashamed of the Gospel*, 281–82. Of course, in the brave new world of electronic lectionary-based aids and "apps," practical definitions and possible abuses of both the term and the concept of a lectionary abound.

20. Goldingay, "Canon and Lection," 97.

has the function of drawing persons into the Eucharistic fellowship. This is really the basic organizing principle behind the Lectionary."[21] According to Horace T. Allen Jr., the "assumed context" of the lectionary is "the un-Protestant (though not un-Reformed) weekly union of Word and Sacrament."[22] He subsequently lists the "[i]ntegration of the sermon into the whole liturgy for the day, and particularly in relation to the celebration of sacraments and pastoral offices" as the last of six "underlying assumptions and principles of selection of liturgical and calendrical contexts."[23] But this in no way diminishes the prominence he gives this consideration in declaring it the first of two recent developments that mark a new era in Christian preaching, namely, the "broadly based consensus to be found in contemporary worship books and directories for worship concerning the use of historically normative weekly celebration of both Word *and* Sacrament on the Lord's Day." Indeed, appeal is made to the "early Christian assumption that the Lord's Day was always to be observed by both spoken and enacted proclamation of the Word of God, as the only appropriate way to participate in the presence of the risen Lord."[24] The second of these two developments, according to Allen, is that preachers, "both Catholic and Protestant, now find themselves in the presence of an ecumenically acceptable system, or 'lectionary,' for determining the choice and arrangement of scripture for the Sunday celebration."[25]

Surely we can take the proponents of the lectionary at their word when they claim the introduction of the various lectionaries—the Roman *Lectionary for Mass* (1969), the *Common Lectionary*, and the *Revised*

---

21. Cited by Bower, "Introduction," 30. See also Trotter, "Are We Preaching a Subversive Lectionary?" 1–2. Although I think the mainline church has surfeited for too long on just this sort of unfiltered, collectivist rhetoric and communitarian ideology at the expense of God's poignant passion for and love of the individual, I assume that Trotter means that individual salvation does indeed happen, just not in total isolation from the larger theater of God's redeeming action on behalf of his elect people. Meanwhile, see a similar expression of the drawing power of preaching, i.e., under the agency of the risen Christ in the preaching moment, in Slemmons, *Groans of the Spirit*, 111.

22. Allen, "Using the Consensus Lectionary," 267.

23. Allen, "Introduction: Preaching in a Christian Context," 3. The other principles, according to Allen, are: (1) Sunday preaching is sequential; (2) Scripture serves as it own context; (3) Scripture governs the liturgical calendar; (4) the preacher is to be "'obedient' to the text rather than choosing it for his or her own purposes"; and (5) preaching is more participatory, both programmatically and ecumenically.

24. Ibid., 1.

25. Ibid., 1–2.

Common Lectionary—has meant an expansion of preaching texts by comparison to practice that was current at the time.[26] Undoubtedly, the increase in lectionary use is hailed as a homecoming to biblical preaching by many.

Unfortunately, the prevailing eucharistic emphasis fails to do justice to several other theological and practical considerations:

First, despite Calvin's ideal of weekly communion, the Liturgy of the Word still predominates in practice over the Liturgy of the Upper Room in a vast number of Reformed congregations for some forty Sundays per year (where the Lord's Supper is celebrated monthly); in other words, the *RCL* evidently makes no intentional provision whatsoever for selecting texts for preaching services where the Supper is not celebrated. On the contrary, Allen asserts that "the reading of the Bible in public worship restores the Scriptures to their primary context as doxological documents, rather than didactic ones."[27] Since doxology is the ultimate aim of eschatological worship, the need for preaching that teaches, admonishes, corrects, trains, and equips the saints (2 Tim 3:16–17) is somehow reduced in the estimation of the designers of the lectionary, as though God could be duly glorified even where his people lack vision or perish in ignorance (see Prov 29:18, KJV et al.).[28] On the contrary, in the seminal preaching scene in Nehemiah, the understanding of the people is emphasized repeatedly (8:2, 3, 7, 8), such that "all the people went their way to eat and drink and to send portions and to make great rejoicing, *because they had*

26. Allen writes, "Most preachers who take on the responsibility of working consistently with the lectionary soon become painfully aware of how little of the canon they were using when the principle of selection was entirely their own interests and favorite passages." See Allen, "Introduction," 17.

27. At this point, it seems to me that Allen comes very close to replacing a Reformed instrumental understanding of Scripture, whereby doxology and revelation are a matter of how the Scriptures are used, with an ontological and idolatrous claim for the glory of the creaturely form of the Scriptures themselves, which I am sure is not what he intends. Allen, "Using the Consensus Lectionary," 268.

28. Eugene Lowry expresses a similar concern when he numbers the very "thematic unity" of the lectionary, with which he has "a love-hate relationship," on the liability side of his scorecard. See Lowry, *Living with the Lectionary*, 11. Lowry's concerns have to do precisely with the overarching *liturgical* (eucharistic), *doxological*, and *anamnetic* aims and the *thematic* results of lectionary design. In short, *preaching (homiletics)* is clearly *not* among its primary aims: "In short, liturgical interest, particularly doxological and anamnetic, have dominated lectionary text selection, and in the process have produced a kind of thematic unity of the lectionary which does not bode well for the preaching office." Ibid., 16.

understood the words that were declared to them" (Neh 8:12; emphasis mine). There is no sense whatsoever that the celebratory meal superseded the need for understanding.

Second, the eucharistic emphasis of the *RCL*, with its implicit eschatological trajectory, occurs in nearly total isolation from the Bible's apocalyptic texts. In fact, the eschatological character of the meal, and of worship in general, is largely overlooked, or at best reduced to socialistic terms, in the literature that has introduced and advocates for the lectionary.[29] In other words, the *RCL* places nearly all the burden for eschatological revelation on the Lord's Supper, reserving to the table liturgy the primary responsibility for speaking on this subject. But such a substitution of the Sacrament for the Word effectively muzzles prophetic preaching in any futuristic sense and has in fact undermined the strength and credibility of mainline churches in apocalyptic times.

Third, in its acrobatic preference for positive texts and its gymnastic avoidance of difficult passages, especially those that call for repentance, the *RCL* seeks to make the Word of God inoffensive and loses sight of the broader (and largely hostile) cosmological reality out of which the church is drawn into the presence of God, and into which it is sent forth as "the church militant."[30] In this respect, Bryan D. Spinks' criticism of the early

29. While Sanders raises certain eschatological questions in "Canon and Calendar," 257–63, Allen complains that Sanders does so "without helpful resolution." Yet Allen's rejoinder that eschatology "is intensively dealt with in the Advent lectionary" is absurdly inadequate; see Allen, "Using the Consensus Lectionary," 267. As for his thoroughly social understanding of the church's mission, Allen writes, "if in our day, the church is finding a new unity around the table of the Word, that can only be for the sake of its social mission, which is dedicated to serving the unity of all, in justice and freedom." Ibid., 265.

30. Louis Berkhof, in writing of the "many-sided character of the church," distinguished between the militant and the triumphant church in this way: "The Church in the present dispensation is a militant Church, that is, she is called unto, and is actually engaged in, a holy warfare. This, of course, does not mean that she must spend her strength in self-destroying internecine struggles, but that she is duty bound to carry on an incessant warfare against the hostile world in every form in which it reveals itself, whether in the Church or outside of it, and against all spiritual forces of darkness. The Church may not spend all her time in prayer and meditation, however necessary and important these may be, nor may she rest on her oars in the peaceful enjoyment of her spiritual heritage. She must be engaged with all her might in the battles of her Lord, fighting in a war that is both offensive and defensive. If the Church on earth is the militant Church, the Church in heaven is the triumphant Church. There the sword is exchanged for a palm of victory, the battle cries are turned into songs of triumph, and the cross is replaced by the crown. The strife is over, the battle is won, and the saints reign with Christ forever and ever. In these two stages of her existence, the Church reflects the humiliation and exaltation of

work of the Joint Liturgical Group's lectionary, namely, "for focusing on God's kindness and avoiding God's severity," applies to the *RCL* as well.[31]

Fourth, and perhaps most telling, is the bald admission by Allen that the Sunday lections were never meant to cover the *whole* canon, but that task belongs to the daily lectionary or the Daily Office.[32] What he fails to recognize is the sense in which, short of a thoroughgoing resurrection of the cathedral office, the balance of the canon (that which is excluded from the *RCL*) will only ever exercise influence in private devotions, not public worship and theology. It is not only Protestants who should ask, How many laypeople go to church every day? How many congregations offer daily public worship? How many individual mainline Christians read the daily lectionary? Undoubtedly, many do. But, equally beyond dispute, far more do not! Yet, the designers of the three-year *RCL* seem quite content with this arrangement. *For this reason alone, preachers must realize that, unless some other schedule of readings such as Year D is provided, no such rectifying tool is to be expected from the designers of the RCL.*

Lastly, despite the sense in which the lectionary provides for some measure of continuity in preaching from week to week, there is no clear priority placed on the need for a homiletical recapitulation of the Christian narrative as a whole. In the same way that the lectionary assumes the Table must bear the (*proleptic*) weight of eschatological revelation, so too is it laden with the primary responsibility for (*anamnetic*) recapitulation.[33] But this point needs further elaboration.

---

her heavenly Lord." See Berkhof, *Systematic Theology*, 565.

31. Spinks, "Christian Worship or Cultural Incantations?" 6–7. Cited by Goldingay, 97. Among other things, the Joint Liturgical Group was responsible for the two-year lectionary that appeared in the *Book of Common Order* (1979) of the Church of Scotland, and provided for a commencement of the church calendar five weeks prior to Advent, with a focus on creation and the formation of the nation of Israel. A reconstituted JLG 2 later produced *A Four Year Lectionary* (1990), which retained this innovation, but failed to garner much ecumenical support as an alternative to the *Common Lectionary* (1983) or to overcome criticism of its earlier model as being too thematic, too narrow, too lacking in narrative selections, etc.

32. Allen, "Using the Consensus Lectionary," 266–67.

33. Clearly this responsibility must be borne by the service of worship as a whole. In the passage noted above, for instance, Berkhof distinguishes perhaps too starkly between prayer and the missionary militancy of the church, for what is crucial is precisely the intersection between them, the point at which worship entails entrance by means of *baptism* (with its attendant dynamics of repentance, confession, renunciation, exorcism, death, burial, and, finally, resurrection with Christ), and prayer, supplication, interces-

RECAPITULATION IS ESSENTIAL

In the most basic sense, to recapitulate (*anakephalaiousthai*) means to sum up, or to gather up. Thus, Paul writes, "The commandments . . . *are summed up* in this word, 'Love your neighbor as yourself'" (Rom 13:9). In a larger Christological sense, the concept of recapitulation has its scriptural roots in Ephesians: "With all wisdom and insight (God) has made known to us the mystery of his will, according to his good pleasure that he set forth in Christ, as a plan for the fullness of time, *to gather up* [*recapitulate*] all things in him, things in heaven and things on earth. In Christ we have also obtained an inheritance, having been destined according to the purpose of him who accomplishes all things according to his counsel and will, so that we, who were the first to set our hope on Christ, might live for the praise of his glory" (Eph 1:8b–12).[34] At root, however, to recapitulate entails (literarily speaking) to place a summary heading over a "chapter," topic, or locus, or even more literally, to give something—or someone?— "a new head," so to speak: arguably the desired effect of every sermon and every worship service!

Goldingay, whose concerns we registered above, is but one among a host of witnesses who insist that recapitulation of "scripture as a whole" is an essential aspect and aim of every service of worship. James A. Sanders, one of the most outspoken critics of the lectionary, argued that the *Common Lectionary* confined salvation history to the first century and thus lost sight of God's saving action throughout history; further, it failed to provide for *lectio continua* through entire books. Sanders also suggested that Israel's long-established practice of systematically reading through the entire Torah is sufficient precedent to warrant a lectionary that includes the entire canon, and only in this way might lectionary preaching properly honor the whole canon as God's story.[35]

Recapitulation is also a major theme in the writings of the late Robert E. Webber, who served as professor of theology at Wheaton College and

---

sion, and doxology become the very occasion for the Spirit's own *recapitulation* of the created order, literally, a removal of Satan as ruler (*arconta*) of the power of the air (Eph 2:1–2) and the reestablishment and exaltation of Christ as head (*kephalen*) of the church (Eph 1:22).

34. But see also the doctrine of the headship of Christ in Colossians: "He is the head [*kephale*] of the body, the church; he is the beginning [*arche*], the firstborn from the dead, so that he might come to have first place in everything" (Col 1:18).

35. Sanders, "Canon and Calendar," 257–63.

director of the Institute for Worship Studies. In the conclusion to what Webber well knew (owing to his terminal illness) would be his last book, *Ancient-Future Worship*, he retraced the major stepping-stones in his own liturgical development, emphasizing the sense in which worship must recapitulate and "do" God's story. In particular, Webber, citing John Meyendorff, called for Eastern Byzantine theology of *creation-incarnation-recreation*, which emphasizes Christ as "new Adam," to supplement the classical Western emphasis (per Augustine, Calvin, and evangelical theology) on creation-sin-redemption.[36] Webber drew on the patristic theme—in Athanasius, *On the Incarnation*, and Irenaeus, in *Against Heresies* and *On the Apostolic Preaching*—of *Christus Victor* as recovered and "recapped" by Gustav Aulén.[37] In fact, part 1 of *Ancient-Future Worship* ends with Webber's poignant *plea* for the church to "recover the *Christus Victor* theme that God in Christ has defeated all the powers of evil, that he has conclusively abolished sin, death, and all that is evil in the world, and that because of his death and resurrection, he will return for his final victory over all that is evil and set up his kingdom and reign over all the earth."[38]

According to Webber's own summation of Irenaeus, Christ brings about the *recapitulation* of all things through his *incarnation, crucifixion* (obedience), and *resurrection*. *Christus Victor* "provides the Christian with an interpretation of all reality. It speaks of the origin of all things; it deals with the problem of evil; it affirms a God who is involved in the created order; it answers the human quest for meaning; it provides hope

36. Webber, *Ancient-Future Worship*, 169.

37. In the second chapter of his classic, *Christus Victor*—a chapter devoted to Irenaeus—Aulén writes, "the point of crucial importance for" Irenaeus, whose "attitude . . . represents the main line of patristic thought" is that "it is God Himself, and not any intermediary, who in Christ accomplishes the work of redemption, and *overcomes sin, death, and the devil*. . . . The Divine victory accomplished in Christ stands in the centre of Irenaeus' thought, and forms the central element in the *recapitulatio*, the restoring and perfecting of the creation, which is his most comprehensive theological idea. The Recapitulation does not end with the triumph of Christ over the enemies which had held (humankind) in bondage; it continues in the work of the Spirit in the church. . . . But the Recapitulation is not realized in this life: Irenaeus' outlook is strongly eschatological, and the gift of the Spirit in this life is for him the earnest of future glory. It remains true, however, that in the process of the restoring and perfecting of creation—for both are involved—the central and the crucial point is the victory of Christ over the hostile powers." Aulén, *Christus Victor*, 21–22; emphasis mine.

38. Webber, *Ancient-Future Worship*, 86.

for the future."[39] In Webber's view, this dominant early view of the atonement is needed as a corrective to the Catholic view of sacrificial mass. All of these exemplify what Webber called a theology of recapitulation and informed his view that worship should retell or "recap" the story of what God has done and continues to do for us on a grand scale.[40]

In short, the point Webber chose to reiterate in his final written witness is simply that God is *the* protagonist of history, and some provision must be made for retelling the whole sweeping story of God's victory in Christ each time the congregation assembles for worship. Though it bears the weight of a last will and testament by a leading liturgical scholar, the centrality of *recapitulation* is not of Webber's own invention.

Perhaps the leading Reformed liturgical scholar of the twentieth century, Jean-Jacques von Allmen devoted the first chapter of his staple textbook to "Christian Worship [understood] as the Recapitulation of the History of Salvation." He cites a Christmas sermon of Lancelot Andrewes (1555–1626), in which the preacher ("successively Bishop of Chichester, Ely, and Winchester") declares, "as there is a recapitulation of all in heaven and earth in Christ, so there is a recapitulation of all in Christ in the holy Sacrament"; but lest we be misled into assigning recapitulation to the sacrament alone, von Allmen adds: "The worship of the Church would be thus a recapitulation of the major event in the history of salvation and so, implicitly, of the whole history of salvation."[41]

It is not my aim to suppress or diminish the sacraments in relation to the preaching of the Word, but simply to ensure that our practice of text selection corresponds to the theological and practical realities that exist in the church, and to do so as far as possible in accordance with the guidance of Scripture. As Barth (following Calvin) said,

> The weakness today is that we do not administer the sacraments at Sunday worship. *In practice baptism ought to come at the beginning of the service—in the presence of the congregation—and Communion at the end. The sermon would then have its meaningful place in the middle between the two.* Of a service of this kind it

39. Ibid., 61.

40. In an earlier iteration of this concern, Webber identifies the *Christus Victor* theme not only in Irenaeus, but in Tertullian, in the *Apostolic Tradition* of Hippolytus (AD 215), and in the Easter sermon of Melito of Sardis (AD 195). See Webber, *Ancient-Future Faith*, esp. ch. 6, "The Theology of Recapitulation."

41. Von Allmen, *Worship*, 32.

could then rightly be said: *recte administrare sacramenta et pure docere evangelium*. But so long as we do not grasp what Evangelical worship is *in its entirety*, our theological efforts, including the liturgical movement, will be invalid. Only when there is true worship with both sermon and sacrament can the liturgy be given its rightful place, for only then can it fulfill its purpose, namely, to lead up to the sacrament.[42]

In other words, for Barth, it is the role of the liturgy as a whole, not the particular burden of the sermon, to lead to the sacrament. Neither should we lose track of this marvelous passage:

How are Word and sacrament related to one another? . . . The Word has been the first and will remain the first. We do not read: Heaven and earth shall pass away but my sacraments shall not pass away; we read: But my words shall not pass away. And just because it is easy for an over-evaluation of the sacraments to enter in among us, since one expects a magical effect from them, it is essential that one consider the sober Evangelical concept as between them. *The Word is the primary thing. The Word existed before the sacrament was.* The Word stands alone, the sacrament cannot stand alone. The Word is God's original essence, the sacrament is first aroused by our need. The Word will remain after our need, the sacrament will disappear after our need. *This presupposed,* I must say that the Word is the audible sacrament and the sacrament is the visible Word. The Word was before the sacrament and exists without the sacrament and will also still exist afterwards.[43]

More recently, Thomas Long has written:

A classically shaped Christian worship service is formed by the biblical story; it is in essence a recapitulation of the sacred narrative of God's interactions with human beings. When the prayer of confession is prayed, Isaiah says once again, "Woe is me, for I am a man of unclean lips." When the Bible is opened, the faithful are once again at Sinai, once again at the Mount of Revelation. When a new convert steps into the waters of baptism, the people of God cross the Red Sea once again, Jesus is baptized in the Jordan once more. When the bread is broken and the wine is poured in the Lord's Supper, the congregation is there in the Upper Room, there at the cross, "for as often as you eat this bread and drink this cup,

42. Barth, *Homiletics*, 59–60; emphasis mine.

43. Rupprecht, *Herman Bezzel als Theologe*, 369. Cited in Barth, *CD* 1/1, 71; my emphasis.

you show forth the Lord's death." To go through the order of worship is symbolically to walk through the whole narrative of faith. The service is a metaphor constantly pointing to its referent.[44]

Marva Dawn, for her part, urges use of the liturgical year to aid us to "bless the Lord more fully."[45] She and Robert Webber both insist that we must seek and find our place in God's story, rather than try to fit God's story into our own.[46] Underlying this assertion is the undeniable reality that God's is the larger narrative, and worship must tell *that* story as *comprehensively* as possible.

As Don Saliers asserts, "every period of reform and renewal has stressed the need to recover in *fullness* the corporate memories of the Church."[47] Likewise, according to John Stott, we should, in our weekly preaching, "gradually unfold 'the whole counsel of God'" so that people can grasp "the fourfold biblical scheme of creation, fall, redemption *and consummation*."[48]

Above all, what is needed is an ever-increasing vision of the biggest of big pictures, an ability to recapitulate, not merely the individual sermon[49] or series of sermons, but the grand story of redemption in a nutshell. Recapitulation requires the preacher to paint the sky, so to speak, to replace a worldview dominated by preoccupation with identity politics—and distorted by sin, death, the devil, and the principalities and the powers of this present darkness (Eph 6:14)—with a summary display or proclamation of the sovereignty of God, the victory of Christ, and the new life in the Spirit. The weekly labors of the preacher and designer of worship begin with the selection of texts that serve as spiritual reminders of God's dramatic revelation of redemption and new creation, all of which finds its proper "head" (Col 1:18) and bodily coherence (1:17) in Christ. As Bartow reminds the reader of Scripture in public worship, "Christ Jesus, crucified, risen, regnant, as attested by the Spirit in Scripture, is the Canon within the canon, the

---

44. Long, *Beyond the Worship Wars*, 10.

45. Dawn, *How Shall We Worship?*, 25–35.

46. Dawn, *Reaching Out without Dumbing Down*, 254–59.

47. Saliers, *Worship and Spirituality*, 22.

48. Stott, *Between Two Worlds*, 170–71; my emphasis.

49. See, e.g., Phelps, *Theory of Preaching*, 520–23.

Norm of norms."[50] This obligates the servant of the Word, the steward of God's mysteries (1 Cor 4:1), to become ever more familiar with the full breadth and scope of Scripture, and ever more adept at recapitulating "the Word" in the fullest sense, in fresh, concise, and memorable ways, such as we do at the table, certainly, when we proclaim, *Christ has died! Christ is risen! Christ will come again!*—but potentially in every liturgical element as well (e.g., the confession and assurance, the profession of faith) and, above all, in the sermon.

RECAPITULATION IS UNAVOIDABLY SELECTIVE

On the downside, the inevitable and unavoidable difficulty inherent in every attempt at recapitulation is that it is by definition selective, and this liability is obviously built in to the lectionary's method of *lectio selecta*.

As often as Webber, for instance, stressed the whole spectrum of God's redemption in Christ, from incarnation through resurrection, ascension, the sending of the Spirit, and the return of Christ, just as often he boiled this down (as did Luther) to death/resurrection, or in a word, baptism.[51] The question that must be put to such shorthand distillations, however, is whether death and resurrection together sufficiently recapitulate the "career" of Christ, or whether, as Stott's fourfold summary (above) reminds us, we need to give more attention to texts that speak of his ascension and return. If the Supper is indeed a foretaste of the heavenly banquet, how are we to understand our (present and future tense) participation in Christ where the third part of the threefold eucharistic mystery, "Christ will come again," is concerned? If it is true that, as two of the *RCL*'s most popular psalms declare, the LORD "is coming to judge the earth" (Pss 96:13; 98:9), how is it that our "ecumenically acceptable system" as a whole manages to systematically avoid texts of judgment, paradigmatic prayers of repentance (Psalms 6; 38; 102; Ezra 9; Nehemiah 9; Daniel 9), and apocalyptic texts that speak of the eschatological future? I ask the question not simply for the sake of speculation or argumentation. Since we as preachers and pastors are charged with feeding others at the "proper time" (Matt 24:45–51), I want to know specifically with regard to text selection, specifically with the aim of our being wise and faithful stewards in the fulfillment of this trust.

50. Bartow, *God's Human Speech*, 78.

51. See, e.g., Webber, *Ancient-Future Time*, 26.

Scripture itself, of course, is full of examples of selective recapitulation. The book of Deuteronomy is arguably recapitulation from beginning to end. The establishment or renewal of a covenant always entails some selective recapitulation of events leading up to the decisive moment and the turning point that the covenant represents. The aforementioned prayers of repentance—call them "the confessional nines," if you will—by Ezra, Nehemiah, and Daniel involve substantial recapitulation, with the focus being on God's greatness and mercy and on Israel's sin. Certain historical psalms (18, 78, 89, 105, 106, 135, et al.), as well as the lengthy sermons by Peter, Stephen, and Paul in Acts, all leap over vast amounts of material in order to get to their primary points and issue fresh iterations of communal memory. What, then, is the rule, "the plumb line" (Amos 7:7–9), that serves to correct such biases, even as they occur in Scripture? This is the question we will attempt to answer in the next chapter.

—3—

The Principle of Canonical Comprehensiveness

HOW CAN WE KNOW, IN A WAY THAT IS FREE FROM BIAS AND PREDISPOSI-tion, what the Spirit is saying to the churches? Given that the Bible con-stitutes the instrument through which the Spirit speaks to us, how do we discern which texts are speaking, which are most compelling, timely, and urgent, at any given moment? To respond to these questions we will identify several key principles: prayer, penitence, the preaching presence of Christ, and the personal discipline of searching the Scriptures daily; but for our immediate purposes, the emphasis will fall on one final prin-ciple to which Scripture attests again and again, namely, the principle of canonical comprehensiveness.

PRAYER TO THE HOLY SPIRIT

The first principle to note is that such knowledge and discernment de-pend on none other than the Holy Spirit, who "helps us in our weak-ness; for we do not know how to pray as we ought, but that very Spirit intercedes with sighs too deep for words" (Rom 8:26).[1] In short, if the Spirit aids us in our weakness and ignorance with respect to prayer, how much more should we be assured that the same Spirit of Truth helps us when we prayerfully go about the task of selecting texts to be expounded and proclaimed in the name of Christ, the Way, Truth, and Life? In short, what von Allmen said of preaching generally—"There is no true preach-

1. See Slemmons, *Groans of the Spirit*, 77, 106.

ing without epiclesis"[2]—applies just as forcefully to the specific task of text selection: *Faithful text selection entails calling upon the Holy Spirit.*

PENITENCE

Practically speaking, the difficulty with this claim lies not with the Spirit as "sender" of the needed inspiration, but with the preacher as "receiver." The fact is, we are all fallible receivers, both individually and corporately, our frequent appeals to community as the essential check and balance against individualistic distortion notwithstanding. Simply put, we get our signals crossed. Therefore, we must pose the question another way. Absent a cognitively clear sense or a strong gut feeling regarding which text(s) one should preach—which are occasional phenomena for most of us—how do we, in a decent, orderly, and upbuilding way, select passages of Scripture for use in worship and preaching, that is, in a way that will prove faithful over the long haul?

We put the question in these terms because in the Matthean passage cited at the end of the previous chapter, Jesus' saying concerning the wise and faithful servants presupposes the "absence" of the anticipated Master, as well as the fact that this absence may become an occasion for temptation, for the servant to entertain the thought, "My master is delayed," as though the Master could *not* arrive in the very next moment or speak a word that one would rather not hear. It will not do to pay lip service to a Reformed view of Scripture, to hold that the Word of God in written form functions instrumentally, that is, that we hear God speaking to us *through* Scripture, if in fact we develop "an ecumenically acceptable system," even an optional one, that aids and abets our propensity to tune out, silence, or marginalize certain texts.

What checks and balances do we have against the all-too-human tendency on the part of the church itself to repress the voice of God? Our resistance runs deep. After all, the prophetic preaching office itself was inaugurated precisely in response to the unanimous plea of "all the people" of Israel that the LORD should *not* speak to them directly again: "When all the people witnessed the thunder and lightning, the sound of the trumpet, and the mountain smoking, they were afraid and trembled and stood at a distance, and said to Moses, 'You speak to us, and we will

2. Von Allmen, *Preaching and Congregation*, 31; cited in Old, *Patristic Roots of Reformed Worship*, 218.

listen; but do not let God speak to us, or we will die'" (Exod 20:18–19; cf. **Deut 5:22–27**).[3] Astonishingly, the LORD actually consented to this accommodating arrangement, saying to Moses, "I have heard the words of this people, which they have spoken to you; they are right in all that they have spoken. If only they had such a mind as this, to fear me and to keep all my commandments always, so that it might go well with them and with their children forever!" (**Deut 5:28b–29**) Moses' response to the people was one of comfort: "Do not be afraid; for God has come only to test you and to put the fear of him upon you so that you do not sin" (Exod 20:20). In other words, the preaching office originated as an incalculable accommodation based on the fact that the people regarded the LORD with holy fear and reverence that would keep them from sinning and result in intergenerational prosperity.

Obviously, when this reality no longer holds, when the fear of the LORD is attenuated among the people of God, when the holiness of God is ignored or forgotten, when the distinction between sacred and secular is (falsely) said to be obsolete,[4] or when a casual, "come as you are" familiarity becomes the rule in Christian worship, we should not be surprised to learn—from the prophets and, indeed, from the terms of the covenant itself (**Deut 28:15–68; Jdg 2:20; 1 Kgs 11:11; Jer 34:18–20; Ezek 17:11–21; Hos 8:1**)—that all bets are off. If "the fear of the LORD is the beginning of wisdom" (Ps 111:10; **Prov 9:10**; cf. 1:7), it should hardly be surprising that when wisdom has no fear on which to make a beginning, things do *not* go well with Israel and the church as the people of God.

Whenever such a crisis of authority arises, as can only happen when a holy fear of the LORD is diminished or absent, homiletical theorists

---

3. Throughout this chapter, texts that lie outside the three-year *RCL* cycle will be listed in bold typeface. While not all of these texts are included in Year D, many (if not most) of them are. This manner of distinguishing between included and excluded texts will hopefully add emphasis to the thrust of this chapter, namely, to reveal how such a simple principle as paying "greater attention" (**Heb 2:1**) to the canonical totality of divine revelation may be altogether lost, forgotten, or overlooked in the absence of so many texts that call for it explicitly.

4. On the importance of teaching the difference between "the holy and the common, the clean and the unclean," see **Lev 10:10–11; Ezek 22:26; 42:20;** and **44:23**; note in particular the sense in which Ezekiel's vision is futuristic, which undermines the assumption from a New Testament perspective that the categories are obsolete. On a closely related note, Wainwright is correct in maintaining the ongoing necessity of distinguishing between the sacred and the secular or profane, even if the necessity is temporary (pertaining to time and history) and not now absolute. See Wainwright, *Doxology*, 404–10.

rightly turn to Jesus in the search for a reforming ideal, but all too often they draw the wrong conclusions. For every preacher since Moses, the crisis of the preacher's responsibility, dependent as it is on the self-revealing God and vested with but a derivative sense of authority, has been compounded in the realization that apostolic preaching (including text selection) cannot reliably model itself on Jesus' *example* of preaching. There are two primary reasons for this. Put in the broadest possible terms, the first pertains to the content of preaching, the second to its form. First, as the Christ, Jesus faced a paradoxical task that we do not face, namely, having to preaching himself, "Christ crucified," without in fact testifying to himself.[5] In Jesus' own preaching, but not in ours, we see the necessity for the messianic secret (Wrede) and the indirect communication that marked so much of his preaching generally.[6] Second, when Jesus preached, because he was and is "without sin" (Heb 4:15; 2 Cor 5:20–21), he was not therefore encumbered by any sin of his own. Such is clearly not the case for the rest of us.

As basic as this is to Christian doctrine, other than a narrow line running from Kierkegaard to Forsyth, Barth, and Bonhoeffer, modern homiletics has yet to advance beyond the sheepish and ironic admission of this fact,[7] and place it in the foreground of the crisis of the preaching vocation. Having been reminded in chapter 1 of Luther's first thesis (i.e., that the entire Christian life is one of repentance)—not a medieval holdover but the veritable taproot of faithful preaching since the Reformation—we must, finally and with full intentionality, apply this thesis to our modes of text selection. For with the calling to preach, there falls to the preacher, and (humanly speaking) *to the preacher alone*, the responsibility, arguably the most important decision that the preacher is charged with making, for determining the Scripture passage or passages on which he or she will preach the Word that, as the Lutherans say, kills in order to make alive. This is not to say that such a decision is made in sheer autonomy or isolation (for we have already noted the obligatory *epiclesis*), or without

---

5. See John 5–9 (most of which is excluded from the *RCL*) where the requirement of two or three witnesses is repeatedly at issue (5:31–47; 8:12–19).

6. In "Toward a Penitential Homiletic," I treated the issue of indirect vs. direct communication extensively as it was advanced by Kierkegaard and misunderstood by Fred Craddock.

7. The supreme expression of this irony in recent homiletics is, of course, Craddock, *As One Without Authority*.

regard to the collective work of ecumenical bodies, the spiritual needs of congregations, or individual listeners. But it does mean that the preacher must appear alone before the God-man, first as a sinner who *alone* bears responsibility for his or her sin, then as a sinner redeemed by grace, and finally, as a redeemed sinner who serves as a trustee-inmate in the spiritual and ecclesial reformatory of temporal existence.

This is the essence of the preacher's vocational identity, the so-called *ethos* of the preacher who labors in "the Reformed tradition," which—it must be said—has nothing to do with what Kierkegaard called "dabbling in reform," something that those who cannot admit their incompetence are clearly not competent to do.[8] The preacher who is not subjectively a penitent lacks the first qualification for preaching: a sufficiently personal relation to the Sovereign content of the Christian preaching, "the Canon within the canon, the Norm of norms" (Bartow), namely, the Lord Jesus Christ. The Reformation at its core was always and is still (speaking sequentially) *first* about the Sovereign God's reformation of the sinful "subject," *and only subsequently* about the objective reformation of the institutional church and its diverse ways of life. God promised to make the one man Abraham a great nation, he sent the individual Moses to call the people of Israel out of Egypt, he dispatched Jonah to Nineveh, John the Baptist to a "brood of vipers," and Paul to the Areopagites, not the other way around. Yes, the collective church is a witness, but it speaks with one voice, or else its sound is indistinct (**1 Cor 14:6–12**), thus the Spirit sets apart individuals, not committees, to serve as its mouthpiece. Thus, to say, "the preacher alone" means the preacher who exercises personal responsibility, who seeks and regularly appears alone before God, before the crucified God-man, in humble contrition, knowing that Christ has offered atonement for the preacher's own sin—the preacher who understands him or herself as properly penitential is unequivocally "the chief of sinners"—and only then for the sins of the listener, of the church, of the human race, and of the whole created order. This is not to thrust the preacher egocentrically into the center of the universe, but it

---

8. "*The evil in our time is not the established order with its many faults. No, the evil in our time is precisely: this evil penchant for reforming, this flirting with wanting to reform,* . . . this hypocrisy of avoiding the consciousness of one's own incompetence by being busy with the diversion of wanting to reform the Church, which our age is least of all competent to do." See Kierkegaard, *Judge for Yourself!*, 212–13; and *Moment and Late Writings*, xxiv.

is to willingly "go and sit down at the lowest place" (Luke 14:10)—to say with the Baptizer, "He must increase, but I must decrease" (**John 3:30**). Only in this way can the preacher seek a fresh word of conviction (in the double sense of both negative conviction of sin and positive conviction of faith and truth) to speak to those with whose spiritual nurture he or she has been commissioned by the Holy Spirit. In sum, both *penitence* and *prayer* are essential and inescapable aspects of the responsibility for the text selection that falls to the preacher each and every time the preacher has occasion to bring a word from the Lord.

THE PREACHING PRESENCE OF JESUS CHRIST

The good news for preaching (with which many preachers have yet to come to terms) and the proper way of understanding the homiletical turn to Jesus, as preachers from Heinrich Bullinger to Dietrich Bonhoeffer have reminded us, is that the risen Christ whom we preach preaches in the same instant. The *presence of Christ* is the effective "change agent," the divine and the divinely competent partner in preaching. So text selection really is a matter of what the Spirit of the risen Christ is saying to the churches! As Richard Lischer has stated, "*Jesus* the Word" is so identified in the New Testament "with the word of preaching, that the one proclaimed *once again* becomes the proclaimer."[9] It is "Jesus himself who is the preacher, blessing our sermons with his presence."[10] Much more could and perhaps should be said on the kerygmatic real presence of Christ in the preaching moment, but for our present purposes we must be content to recommend the work of James F. Kay, along with (again) a rich vein of Lutheran homiletics from Dietrich Bonhoeffer, to Gerhard Forde, to David J. Lose.[11]

THE PERSONAL DISCIPLINE OF DAILY SCRIPTURE READING

To these rules, we must add a fourth, or at least make explicit an assumption that has been with us all along, namely, the necessity for *regular (daily), disciplined, and thorough searching of the Scriptures*. Of the preacher's

9. Lischer, *Theology of Preaching*, 55; emphasis mine.

10. Ibid., 56.

11. Kay, *Christus Præsens*; Fant, *Bonhoeffer*; Forde, *Theology Is for Proclamation*; Lose, *Confessing Jesus Christ*.

many responsibilities, this is clearly one of a relatively small number that must be deemed essential.[12] As we consider how the Spirit guides the preacher to a fitting text for any given preaching occasion, we by no means rule out the possibility, even the likelihood, that the Spirit makes use of daily and weekly lectionaries, as may well have been the case on that Sabbath when Jesus himself preached in the synagogue at Nazareth. On the contrary, we can be assured of finding ourselves on solid ground if we bear in mind this rule, given by the Living Word himself: "the Advocate, the Holy Spirit, whom the Father will send in my name, will teach you *everything*, and remind you of *all* that I have said to you" (John 14:26). In other words, if we hear the Spirit speaking through the Scripture with the aim of thoroughness and comprehensive reminding, it is imperative that the minister "shall" have personal devotions, and conduct regular (daily), disciplined, thorough, and comprehensive study of the Scriptures.

But *personal devotional reading of the Scriptures*, in some respects, eventually compounds the crisis of text selection for the preacher. For as the preacher discovers and becomes more familiar with the rich and "lavish" treasures of the Bible through daily, personal devotion, he or she likewise discovers that these texts speak, not only to the preacher's own needs, but to innumerable needs, openings, and opportunities in the church and the world as well. As one's knowledge of Scripture grows, it becomes clear that the world and the church are dying of spiritual and scriptural malnutrition, and that the Word alone has the requisite nourishment to offer that the external and practical constraints placed upon the weekly sermon simply will not accommodate.[13] "One does not live by bread alone, but by *every* word that comes from the mouth of the LORD" (**Deut 8:3**; Matt 4:4).

Thus, with these principles in mind—prayer (*epiclesis* to the Holy Spirit), penitence (subjective and personal reformation on the part of the preacher by the agency of the Spirit and by exercising the gift of repentance), the preaching presence of the risen Christ, and the personal,

---

12. "Those responsible for teaching and preaching the Word have a special responsibility to ensure that in their personal worship they observe *a discipline of reading from the fullness of Scripture*." See W-2.2004 in *BO*; emphasis mine; cf. W-5.3000.

13. Without wishing to actually impose this sort of legalistic demand upon what should be one of the greatest joys of ministry, it is at least worth considering what the possible benefits might be if ministers, in order to maintain their ordination, were required to pass progressively more difficult Bible content exams every five years.

devotional practice of searching the Scriptures—let us proceed to the specific ways in which the Bible attests to the principle of canonical comprehensiveness.

AS A CORRECTIVE TO THE SELECTIVE NATURE OF RECAPITULATION, THE HOLY SPIRIT REPEATEDLY AFFIRMS THE TOTALITY OF THE REVELATION

One can easily imagine many learned objections to upholding the ideal of preaching the whole canon. After all, goes one line of reasoning, not every text has played a liturgical role in the history of Israel and the church. But the more proper question may be, should we not remain open to the possibility that every text may acquire a liturgical role that has not yet discovered one? When (according to Reformed theology) has the argument from extrabiblical tradition ever rightly been the final arbiter? Even if the tradition of having a liturgical role were decisive, why is the book of Deuteronomy not still read in its entirety every seventh year (**Deut 31:10–11**)?

Others might object, citing Augustine (on the problem of soteriology), that sometimes the word *all* does not mean *all*. This simple exegetical point has fueled countless debates concerning salvation,[14] but few, if any, concerning the appropriate breadth of text selection for preaching. The obvious rejoinder to such an objection is simple: more often than not, *all* does indeed mean *all*; and even if there may be a few exceptional moments when *all* does not mean *absolutely* all, *all* most assuredly does (at least) mean *many* or *most*; at the very least *all* suggests we need a more expansive view, one that summons us to pay "greater attention" to something beyond our present field of vision, something that lies nearer (yet within) the known boundaries of the canon.

Still others may object, citing Calvin as perhaps the primary exemplar of *lectio continua* preaching, that even he did not quite complete the task of preaching through the whole canon. But again, the premier example from Christian tradition is no substitute for "the Norm of norms," the Word itself/himself, as Calvin would be the first to admit.

---

14. For Augustine, "all" can mean "many" (*Julian*, iv, 8); or "some of every kind" (*Enchiridion*, c. 103); or it may mean "that God gives everyone at least the desire for salvation," etc. See Farrar, *Mercy and Judgment*, 421 n. 14.

The fact that there remains a body of texts not included even via the present proposal for a fourth year should not obscure the principle on which this expansion is based and which gives direction to it, namely, that the Reformed canon of Scripture is the true standard of the church's "common texts" for preaching.[15] As helpful as is David Kelsey's distinction between "the Christian canon" and a theologian's "working canon"[16] where the church's ministry of preaching is concerned, this distinction needs to be radically reduced and these two views of canon brought closer together. Year D is not a complete solution. While it expands by giant leaps the boundaries of the "working canon," it does not yet reach the boundaries of the "Christian canon"; at best we might say (with a baseball analogy) that with the Psalms, the Gospels, and the Epistles, we become aware of the warning track, so to speak.

By indicating the canon as the proper limit and boundary within which are to be found the church's common texts for preaching, and in appealing to many biblical texts that would appear to support this expansive proposal, I do not intend to make the anachronistic and historically naïve claim that any of the texts cited below speak directly of what would only centuries later be regarded as "the Christian canon" of Scripture. Nevertheless, there are many texts that bear witness to this underlying scriptural principle that (for lack of a better term) we may call "the principle of canonical comprehensiveness." Paradoxical though it may be, this principle or dynamic is at work in a long and persistent series of moments, or a textual pattern, whereby the Word continually *testifies to itself* (in its various genres, guises, and expressions), so to speak, and *demands consideration of its entirety*. This is true despite Scripture's own insistence that two or three witnesses are required for any proper judgment (**Deut**

---

15. As I noted in ch. 1, the historical record regarding the apocryphal books in the Anglo-Catholic canon clearly shows that they are not included in the canon of all Christian denominations, but the authority and canonicity of the sixty-six books of the Reformed biblical tradition are not in dispute; in short, they are already "common" to all denominations and need no further justification or warrants than they received at Nicaea, during the European Reformations, and at Westminster. Neither the Jesus Seminar nor the Consultation on Common Texts has any legitimate theological basis for questioning the authority of any part of these canonical books. On the other hand, I leave it to those in the Anglo-Catholic traditions to consider the merits of lectionary expansion that would include the missing texts from the Apocrypha.

16. Kelsey, *Uses of Scripture in Recent Theology*, 104.

17:6; 19:15; Matt 18:16; 2 Cor 13:1; 1 Tim 5:19; Heb 10:28) and that testimony to oneself is not valid (**John 5:31**; cf. **John 8:13**).[17]

One of the most instructive texts in this regard is, in fact, the seminal passage (**John 5:30–47**), yet another omitted from the *RCL*, wherein the Incarnate Word teaches some Jewish leaders a thing or two about those witnesses, human and divine, that testify to himself:

> Human witness: John the Baptist, embodiment of the prophets (5:33–35)
> The Word Incarnate: the works of Jesus (5:36)
> The heavenly Father (5:37–38)
> The Word written: the Scriptures (5:39–40)
> Human witness: Moses and the Torah (5:45–47)

This testimonial recapitulation, punctuated throughout with Jesus' assertion of the truth of his testimony, hinges on the fact that he himself only teaches what he has been given from the Father to whom he testifies (5:30; cf. 7:16); thus, his testimony is valid "even if" he judges and testifies on his own behalf (8:14, 16), for as Jesus reminds us elsewhere in John's Gospel, "The Father and I are one" (10:30).

The key question of text selection, pneumatically understood, that we must keep before us is: Will we allow the Word of God the freedom to speak on (and in) God's own terms, in God's own time? James A. Sanders' warning that the lectionary "tyrannically" subordinates *canon* to the *calendar* is well taken,[18] but today, with lectionary preaching threatening to monopolize the mainline sector of the homiletical economy, it is far more important that preachers be disabused of the naïve assumption that—in the "absence" of the Master—the latest form of post-Vatican II expansion is innocent, or that it cannot or has not become an instrument of "the 'tyranny of the church' over the Bible";[19] neither should we assume that an

17. A better, more orthodox, less colloquial way of speaking of the self-attestation of the Word, of course, would be to state matters in Trinitarian terms, wherein we recognize that the Spirit and the Father testify to the Word, the Word and Spirit to the Father, and the Father and the Son send the Spirit, which among other things, fulfills the requirement that every testimony be corroborated.

18. Sanders, "Canon and Calendar," 258.

19. See Brueggemann, *Book That Breathes*, 39–40. Admittedly, Brueggemann is not discussing lectionaries in his essay on "Biblical Authority and the Church's Task of Interpretation," but let it be noticed that his distinction between the tyranny of the church over the Bible and the tyranny of the academy over the Bible is much too sharply drawn, for in fact church hierarchies are populated by those who have been credentialed by and place the most stock in the academy; in other words, the two continually reinforce

appeal to the canon as the proper norm for text selection carries with it the sense of "dogmatic closure" that Brueggemann himself associates with the Yale School program of Brevard Childs.

On the contrary, at the risk of alienating some readers, the problem is not that the canon is too restrictive when it comes to the selection of preaching texts (as proponents of the Gnostic Gospels or Bishop John Shelby Spong evidently hold). No, but the lectionary is! The real problem is that so many preachers, to say nothing of the laity, often evince a less-than-thorough knowledge and practice of Scripture itself,[20] with the result that mainline preaching today too often pacifies an increasingly lactose intolerant church with a milky "condensed version" of the Word, in the name of "an ecumenically acceptable system" that effectively, even if not quite or not yet legalistically, reduces the possibility that the church will be disturbed by the Bible's more difficult texts.

Doubtless, the notion of limitation is inherent in the concept of a canon, even at the root level (see 2 Cor 10:12–18); but there can also be no doubt that when it comes to the lectionary and the canon, the latter is the outer limit that has not yet begun to be explored, representing as it does far greater freedom to investigate and inhabit "the strange new world of the Bible" (Barth) and offering far greater revelatory potential for the Spirit to speak a fresh and bracing, yet ultimately revitalizing word in the churches.[21]

In an important passage on the ways in which we are told the purpose of preaching's performative function is a matter of "turning ink into blood," Bartow acknowledges that options can theoretically include deconstructive performance, though he asks concerning those texts that receive no performance at all:

> But what about justice? What about giving voice to the voiceless? What about giving place to the marginalized? Is there a linguistically and socially constructed world more easily dismissed than

---

one another, as is clearly the case with the *RCL*. With that in mind, we would do well to pay far "greater attention" to what Brueggemann has to say about "vested interests" and apply it to lectionary design! See Brueggemann, *Word Militant*, 78.

20. Though Presbyterian seminary students are required to pass a Bible content examination, the passing score is quite low: 70 out of 100. Even then, the passing rate scarcely fosters confidence that Presbyterian ministers enter their pastoral calling with a commanding knowledge of, or fluency in, the Scriptures.

21. Barth, *Word of God and the Word of Man*, 28–50.

one that has had all its blood drawn and turned into ink? Are there voices more easily silenced than the muted voices of literature? Are there human experiences of God more readily kept at the margins of consciousness than those entangled in words translated into living tongues from now dead languages and disputed manuscripts? In the church, the canon of Scripture can hardly be considered monolithic. It speaks with many voices (some of them profoundly in conflict with each other); and, in the end, the church, and not simply individual members of it or parties within it, will decide which voices are ascendant and why.[22] In other words, the church attends to the texts of its canon critically . . . But those varied texts, *given the chance*, can enable unique ways of being in the world to be known, and not just known about, to be seen, heard, felt (imaginatively touched and smelled) as living speech. *When that happens—and only when that happens—the church can understand itself at least to be attempting a faithful engagement of the word and the work of Scripture.*[23]

If I read Bartow aright, the claim he is making here is that the church cannot even begin to attempt (!) to faithfully engage "the word and the work of Scripture" until it gives the canon's forgotten, silenced, and overlooked texts a chance to speak afresh in the worship and the preaching of the church.

How, then, does "the book that breathes new life" (Brueggemann) testify to its own principle of completeness that characterizes faithful and wise stewardship of the Word? How specifically does Scripture advocate for "comprehensive comprehension" and "greater attention" to the entirety of the revelation? Let us count the ways!

22. In light of this, some might suggest the present proposal lacks the proper ecclesiastical qualification since it does not proceed from a committee, consultation, council, or other collective ecumenical body, to which I would reply that it should be understood (1) as suggestive, (2) as an exercise of the explicit constitutional responsibilities of a Minister of Word and Sacrament, now teaching elder, in selecting texts for preaching, and (3) as an offering in the name of Jesus Christ and thus worthy of the same lack of distinction between the individual and the church that Barth observes in, e.g., Luther, Calvin, and the Heidelberg Catechism, on the subject of prayer, specifically, praying the Lord's Prayer; see Barth, *Prayer*, 5–6.

23. Bartow, *God's Human Speech*, 66–67; italics mine. I concede that I am applying Bartow's thought, as I did Brueggemann's, to the problem of the lectionary, which is not explicitly the issue with which either author is concerned.

1. Comprehensiveness Is Couched in Nutritional Terms

The Bible uses a variety of terms in which to call attention to the entirety of the Word. Granted, in any given instance, this nearly always occurs with respect to a particular genre of literature, tables of commandments, body of statutes, collection of prophetic utterances, epistles, sayings of Jesus, etc. But taken together, it can be truly said: "The sum of your word is truth" (**Ps 119:160**).

The need to attend to the totality of the Word is commonly expressed in a host of nutritional metaphors; food, bread, and manna represent the Word of God so widely that it is often taken for granted. This pattern is recognized, among other places, in the temptation of Jesus in the wilderness, when he replies to the devil's first temptation to turn stones into bread: "It is written, 'One does not live by bread alone, but by every word that comes from the mouth of God'" (Matt 4:4). Unfortunately, the same Torah portion to which Jesus refers, wherein we discover the very reason why the LORD sometimes allows his people to undergo deprivation, is not included in the *RCL*: "[The LORD] humbled you by letting you hunger, then by feeding you with manna, with which neither you nor your ancestors were acquainted, in order to make you understand that one does not live by bread alone, but by every word that comes from the mouth of the LORD" (**Deut 8:3**).

So common is this nutritional connection in the minds of the scripturally literate that one recent lectionary-based preaching resource has recently appeared under the title, *Feasting on the Word*, no doubt an allusion to the feeding of the five thousand. But the selection of this metaphor for such a resource begs the question: What about the post-feast "cleanup" task commanded by Jesus? For in the Johannine account of the feeding, Jesus instructs his disciples to "gather up the fragments left over, so that nothing may be lost" (John 6:12). If the preaching of the Word is like this feast, how can we justify neglecting this humble task of gathering up the leftovers, or obscuring it with moralistic interpretations in the name of stewardship of temporal resources—perishable food, worldly possessions, the environment, etc.—when we have yet to apply it to the Word itself? Jesus' instruction here surely applies first and foremost to our stewardship of the (eternal) Word of God, and this, I suggest, means thoroughness in the task of text selection, "so that nothing may be lost."

2. Comprehensiveness Is Expressed Teleologically

One of the reasons it is important to stress the dialectical nature of this undertaking is that the missionary nature of Jesus' statements regarding the law and the prophets, on the one hand, and the gospel, on the other, is so often overlooked. He came to *fulfill* the law and the prophets and will not remove or alter a single stroke of the letter of the law (Matt 5:18; Luke 6:17); yet in so doing he has not instituted a new legalism, but revealed how the law and the prophets prepared the way for the gospel itself. The law cannot be considered fulfilled where either the law itself is diminished—"For whoever keeps the whole law but fails in one point has become accountable for all of it" (Jas 2:10)—or where love is lacking: "Love does no wrong to a neighbor; therefore, love is the fulfilling of the law" (Rom 13:10). "Therefore, whoever breaks one of the least of these commandments, and teaches others to do the same, will be called least in the kingdom of heaven; but whoever does them and teaches them will be called great in the kingdom of heaven" (Matt 5:19).

3. The Need for Comprehensiveness Is Revealed in Light of the Resurrection and in Anticipation Thereof

With the actual fulfillment of the law, the gospel is free to go forth. Yet even in such a familiar passage as the Great Commission, we have overlooked the comprehensiveness with which the church is to teach obedience to, not seek the consultation or ask permission of, the Gentiles: "Go therefore and make disciples of all nations, baptizing them in the name of the Father and of the Son and of the Holy Spirit, and teaching them to obey *everything* that I have commanded you. And remember, I am with you always, to the end of the age" (Matt 28:19–20).

Other resurrection appearances of Jesus uphold the entirety of the revelation writ large. Along the road to Emmaus, for example, the risen Jesus says to Cleopas and his companion, "'Oh, how foolish you are, and how slow of heart to *believe all that the prophets have declared!* Was it not necessary that the Messiah should suffer these things and then enter into his glory?' Then beginning with *Moses and all the prophets,* he interpreted to them the things about himself *in all the scriptures*" (Luke 24:25–27).

Earlier, in his farewell discourse, wherein he anticipates the post-resurrection era (in a text already mentioned above), Jesus promises the gift of the Holy Spirit in such a way as to clearly establish "comprehensive reminding" as a major aspect of the work of the Spirit: "But the Advocate, the Holy Spirit, whom the Father will send in my name, will teach you *everything*, and remind you of *all* that I have said to you" (John 14:26).

4. Comprehensive Revelation Is Nothing Less than the Basis for Friendship with Christ

In the same farewell discourse, Jesus identifies the comprehensiveness of his disclosure as the very reason why he now regards his disciples as his friends: "I do not call you servants any longer, because the servant does not know what the master is doing; but I have called you friends, *because* I have made known to you *everything* that I have heard from my Father" (John 15:15). While it is beyond dispute that Christ's love for those whom he called his friends is expressed supremely in his death on their behalf (15:13), and while his friendship appears conditional (15:14), the causal assertion, "*because* I have made known to you *everything*," clearly establishes a warrant for Jesus' application of the term "friends" to his disciples.[24]

5. Comprehensiveness in the Angelic Commission to the New Testament Church

The arrest of the apostles by the high priest and his minions was but one of many instances in the book of Acts in which forces hostile to the church used intimidation and force to try to silence the gospel. In but the first of a series of divinely orchestrated jailbreaks (12:7–10; 16:25–28; cf. 23:12–35), it becomes clear that God does not intend that the preaching ministry of the church should be restrained or hushed, but that the gospel should go forth in all its fullness; for Luke reports that "during the night an angel of the Lord opened the doors of the jail and brought them out. 'Go, stand in the temple courts,' he said, 'and tell the people *the full message* of this new life'" (Acts 5:19-20).

---

24. Behind this, of course, stands the tradition that Abraham was "called the friend of God" (Jas 2:23; cf. Gen 15:6; 2 Chr 20:7); that "the LORD used to speak to Moses face to face, as one speaks to a friend" (Exod 33:11), and the assertion of the psalmist: "The friendship of the LORD is for those who fear him, and he makes his covenant known to them" (25:14).

6. Comprehensiveness according to a Pauline Theology of the Word

The entirety of the Pauline correspondence aims at making what were the previously hidden mysteries of God fully known in the revelation of Jesus Christ (Rom 1:1–6; 16:25–27), who alone can remove the darkening veil that hardens the minds of those who read the old covenant (2 Cor 3:12–17). But we mention five texts that speak specifically of the full breadth of the revelation.

In perhaps the most comprehensive letter, the Epistle to the Romans, the entirety of what he considered to be Scripture Paul declares to have a clearly instructive, edifying, encouraging, and hopeful purpose: "For *whatever was written* in former days was written for our instruction, so that by steadfastness and by the encouragement of the scriptures we might have hope" (Rom 15:4).

In his most famous pastoral statement regarding Scripture itself, we have this bold assertion of Scripture's inspiration, authority, and comprehensive usefulness: "*All scripture* is inspired by God and is useful for teaching, for reproof, for correction, and for training in righteousness, so that everyone who belongs to God may be proficient, equipped for *every* good work" (2 Tim 3:16–17).

In an epistle that veritably sings with the *pleroma* or "fullness" of the revelation in Christ, the apostle recalls his kerygmatic and missionary vocation in a way that sets the standard for every generation of preachers: "I became its servant according to God's commission that was given to me for you, to make *the word of God fully known*" (Col 1:25).

Although Paul's polemic against righteousness based on the law is well known, this does not stop him, in his appearance before Felix, from appealing to "*everything* laid down according to the law or written in the prophets" as the basis for his "hope in God—a hope that they themselves [Paul's accusers] also accept—that there will be a resurrection of both the righteous and the unrighteous" (Acts 24:14–15).

Lastly, in reference to being "servants of Christ and stewards of God's mysteries" (1 Cor 4:1), Paul asserts the humbling, unifying benefit of observing a sort of proto-canonical limitation to revelation in written form: "I have applied all this to Apollos and myself for your benefit . . . so that you may learn through us the meaning of the saying, 'Nothing beyond what is written,' so that none of you will be puffed up in favor of one against another" (4:6). Difficult as this text may be to interpret with certainty, since even the Jewish canon was scarcely a settled matter when Paul was writing, this very ambiguity illustrates the fact that in each of the above cases, as well as in the texts cited in tabular form below, while the whole revelation to which the text refers may be different (e.g., the Torah, the covenant given at Sinai, the prophets, the sayings of Jesus) depending on the literary setting in question, the historical period, or the developmental stage in God's progressive revelation, these particular "wholes" should be thought of as canons within the Christian canon. What I am proposing is that, taken together, the various objects to which these "wholes" refer form a larger mosaic that sufficiently resembles and corresponds to the entirety of the Reformed canon such that any lack of correspondence between them must be considered negligible, with the assurance that the entire corpus of Scripture is fair game for preaching. I would even go so far as to say that this extends to the consideration of textual variants as, if not historically and critically normative, at least as possibly informative and revelatory for the preparation of sermons. In other words, the "working canon" of the church's preaching should be radically inclusive of all texts in the Christian canon, even if not every verse or variant makes its way from the preacher's desk to the pulpit.

FURTHER EVIDENCE OF THE PRINCIPLE OF CANONICAL COMPREHENSIVENESS

In what remains of this chapter, a sampling of texts that similarly declare the need to attend to the fullness of the revelation will be listed, with evidence of the principle of comprehensiveness emphasized (in italics), but without further elaboration. In considering this compilation, the reader should bear in mind that (1) since we have already mentioned a number of New Testament texts, the preponderance of those listed below will be found in the Old Testament, with particular concentrations in Deuteronomy, in the former prophets, and in the largest of the Torah psalms (Psalm 119); (2) although there are relatively few texts listed from the latter prophets, the forgetfulness of Torah underlies the entirety of this major section of the Old Testament; therefore, whole chapters, episodes, and literary sections (e.g., **Jeremiah 36**) must be read in this light; and (3) if this method of simply listing texts appears gratuitous or tiresome, it will hopefully convince the reader that, though this list is *not* exhaustive (!), the comprehensive principle is no mere matter of idiom or idiosyncrasy, and the resultant list may serve as a point of reference for exegetical explorations beyond the bounds of both the *RCL* and *Year D* itself.

THE TORAH

Exod 6:28–29	On the day when the LORD spoke to Moses in the land of Egypt, he said to him, "*I am the LORD; tell Pharaoh king of Egypt all that I am speaking to you.*"
Exod 7:2	You shall *speak all that I command you*, and your brother Aaron shall tell Pharaoh to let the Israelites go out of his land.
Exod 19:7–8a	So Moses came, summoned the elders of the people, and *set before them all these words* that the LORD had commanded him. The people all answered as one: "*Everything that the LORD has spoken we will do.*"
Exod 23:13	Be attentive to *all* that I have said to you. Do not invoke the names of other gods; do not let them be heard on your lips.
Exod 23:22	But *if you listen attentively to his voice and do all that I say*, then I will be an enemy to your enemies and a foe to your foes.
Lev 19:37	You shall keep *all* my statutes and all my ordinances, and observe them: I am the LORD.
Lev 20:22	You shall keep *all* my statutes and *all* my ordinances, and observe them, so that the land to which I bring you to settle in may not vomit you out.
Lev 26:14–16	But if you will not obey me, and do not observe *all* these commandments, if you spurn my statutes, and abhor my ordinances, so that you will not observe *all* my commandments, and you break my covenant, I in turn will do this to you: I will bring terror on you; consumption and fever that waste the eyes and cause life to pine away. You shall sow your seed in vain, for your enemies shall eat it.
Num 15:40	So you shall remember and *do all my commandments*, and you shall be holy to your God.
Deut 5:29	If only they had such a mind as this, to fear me and *to keep all my commandments always*, so that it might go well with them and with their children forever!
Deut 10:12–13	So now, O Israel, what does the LORD your God require of you? Only to fear the LORD your God, to walk in *all his ways*, to love him, to serve the LORD your God with all your heart and with all your soul, and to keep the commandments of the LORD your God and his decrees that I am commanding you today, for your own well-being.

Deut 12:28, 32	*Be careful to obey all these words that I command you to-day*, so that it may go well with you and with your children after you forever, because *you will be doing what is good and right in the sight of the* LORD *your God.* . . . *You must diligently observe everything that I command you; do not add to it or take anything from it.*
Deut 27:1	Then Moses and the elders of Israel charged all the people as follows: *Keep the entire commandment* that I am commanding you today.
Deut 28:1	If you will only obey the LORD your God, by *diligently observing all his commandments* that I am commanding you today, the LORD your God will set you high above all the nations of the earth.
Deut 28:14–15	. . . and if you do not turn aside from *any of the words that I am commanding you* today, either to the right or to the left, following other gods to serve them. But if you will not obey the LORD your God by diligently observing *all* his commandments and decrees, which I am commanding you today, then *all* these curses shall come upon you and overtake you.
Deut 28:58–59	If you do not *diligently observe all the words of this law* that are written in this book, fearing this glorious and awesome name, the LORD your God, then the LORD will overwhelm both you and your offspring with severe and lasting afflictions and grievous and lasting maladies.
Deut 29:29	The secret things belong to the LORD our God, but the revealed things belong to us and to our children forever, to *observe all the words of this law.*
Deut 30:8–9a	Then you shall again obey the LORD, *observing all his commandments* that I am commanding you today, and the LORD your God will make you abundantly prosperous in all your undertakings, in the fruit of your body, in the fruit of your livestock, and in the fruit of your soil.
Deut 31:12	Assemble the people—men, women, and children, as well as the aliens residing in your towns—so that they may hear and learn to fear the LORD your God and to *observe diligently all the words of this law.*
Deut 31:24	When Moses had finished writing down in a book *the words of this law to the very end* . . .

Deut 32:44-47	Moses came and *recited all the words of this song* in the hearing of the people, he and Joshua son of Nun. When Moses had finished *reciting all these words* to all Israel, he said to them: "*Take to heart all the words* that I am giving in witness against you today; give them as a command to your children, so that they may *diligently observe all the words of this law*. This is no trifling matter for you, but rather your very life; through it you may live long in the land that you are crossing over the Jordan to possess."

The Former Prophets (including Chronicles)

Josh 1:7-8	Only be strong and very courageous, being careful to *act in accordance with all the law* that my servant Moses commanded you; do not turn from it to the right hand or to the left, so that you may be successful wherever you go. This book of the law shall not depart out of your mouth; you shall meditate on it day and night, so that you may *be careful to act in accordance with all that is written in it*. For then you shall make your way prosperous, and then you shall be successful.
Josh 1:16-18	They answered Joshua: "*All* that you have commanded us we will do, and wherever you send us we will go. Just as we obeyed Moses in *all* things, so we will obey you. Only may the Lord your God be with you, as he was with Moses! Whoever rebels against your orders and disobeys your words, *whatever you command*, shall be put to death. Only be strong and courageous."
Josh 8:34-35	And afterward he *read all the words of the law*, blessings and curses, according to *all that is written in the book of the law*. There was *not a word of all that Moses commanded that Joshua did not read* before all the assembly of Israel, and the women, and the little ones, and the aliens who resided among them.
Josh 22:2	[Joshua] said to them, "You have *observed all that Moses* the servant of the Lord *commanded you*, and have obeyed me in *all that I have commanded* you."
Josh 23:6-8	Therefore be very steadfast to *observe and do all that is written in the book of the law of Moses*, turning aside from it neither to the right nor to the left, so that you may not be mixed with these nations left here among you, or make mention of the names of their gods, or swear by them, or serve them, or bow yourselves down to them, but hold fast to the Lord your God, as you have done to this day.

Josh 23:14–15	"And now I am about to go the way of all the earth, and you know in your hearts and souls, all of you, that *not one thing has failed of all the good things that the* LORD *your God promised concerning you; all have come to pass for you, not one of them has failed.* But just as *all the good things that the* LORD *your God promised* concerning you have been fulfilled for you, so the LORD will bring upon you *all the bad things,* until he has destroyed you from this good land that the LORD your God has given you."
Josh 24:27	Joshua said to all the people, "See, this stone shall be a witness against us; for it has heard *all the words of the* LORD that he spoke to us; therefore it shall be a witness against you, if you deal falsely with your God."
1 Sam 3:12	"On that day I will fulfill against Eli *all that I have spoken concerning his house, from beginning to end.*"
1 Sam 8:10	So Samuel reported *all the words of the* LORD to the people who were asking him for a king.
1 Kgs 6:11–12	Now the word of the LORD came to Solomon, "Concerning this house that you are building, if you will walk in my statutes, obey my ordinances, and keep *all* my commandments by walking in them, then I will establish my promise with you, which I made to your father David."
1 Kgs 9:4; cf. 2 Chr 7:17	"As for you, if you will walk before me, as David your father walked, with integrity of heart and uprightness, doing according to *all* that I have commanded you, and keeping my statutes and my ordinances . . ."
1 Kgs 11:38	"If you will listen to *all that I command you,* walk in my ways, and do what is right in my sight by keeping my statutes and my commandments, as David my servant did, I will be with you, and will build you an enduring house, as I built for David, and I will give Israel to you."
2 Kgs 21:8	"I will not cause the feet of Israel to wander any more out of the land that I gave to their ancestors, if only they will be careful to do according to *all* that I have commanded them, and according to *all* the law that my servant Moses commanded them."
2 Kgs 22:13	[Josiah speaking]: "Go, inquire of the LORD for me, for the people, and for all Judah, concerning *the words of this book that has been found;* for great is the wrath of the LORD that is kindled against us, *because our ancestors did not obey the words of this book, to do according to all that is written concerning us.*"

2 Kgs 22:16	[Huldah speaking]: Thus says the LORD, I will indeed bring disaster on this place and on its inhabitants—*all the words of the book that the king of Judah has read.*
2 Kgs 23:2	The king went up to the house of the LORD, and with him went all the people of Judah, all the inhabitants of Jerusalem, the priests, the prophets, and all the people, both small and great; he read in their hearing *all the words of the book of the covenant that had been found* in the house of the LORD.
2 Kgs 23:25	Before [Josiah] there was no king like him, who turned to the LORD with all his heart, with all his soul, and with all his might, *according to all the law of Moses*; nor did any like him arise after him.
1 Chr 17:20–21	There is no one like you, O LORD, and there is no God besides you, *according to all that we have heard with our ears.* Who is like your people Israel, one nation on the earth whom God went to redeem to be his people, making for yourself a name for great and terrible things, in driving out nations before your people whom you redeemed from Egypt?
1 Chr 28:8	Now therefore in the sight of all Israel, the assembly of the LORD, and in the hearing of our God, *observe and search out all the commandments of the LORD your God*; that you may possess this good land, and leave it for an inheritance to your children after you for ever.
2 Chr 33:7–8	The carved image . . . that (Manasseh) had made he set in the house of God, of which God said to David and to his son Solomon, "In this house, and in Jerusalem, which I have chosen out of all the tribes of Israel, I will put my name forever; I will never again remove the feet of Israel from the land that I appointed for your ancestors, *if only they will be careful to do all that I have commanded them, all the law, the statutes, and the ordinances given through Moses.*"
2 Chr 34:30	The king [Josiah] went up to the house of the LORD, with all the people of Judah, the inhabitants of Jerusalem, the priests and the Levites, all the people both great and small; he read in their hearing *all the words of the book of the covenant* that had been found in the house of the LORD.

THE WRITINGS AND THE PSALMS

Job 33:1	[Elihu speaking]: "But now, hear my speech, O Job, and listen to *all my words*."
Ps 18:21–24	For I have kept the ways of the LORD, and have not wickedly departed from my God. For *all his ordinances* were before me, and his statutes I did not put away from me. I was blameless before him, and I kept myself from guilt. Therefore the LORD has recompensed me according to my righteousness, according to the cleanness of my hands in his sight.
Ps 19:7	*The law of the LORD is perfect*, reviving the soul; the decrees of the LORD are sure, making wise the simple . . .
Ps 111:7–8	The works of his hands are faithful and just; *all his precepts* are trustworthy. They are *established forever and ever*, to be performed with faithfulness and uprightness.
Ps 119:6	Then I shall not be put to shame, having my eyes fixed on *all your commandments*.
Ps 119:13	With my lips I declare *all the ordinances of your mouth*.
Ps 119:86	*All your commandments* are enduring; I am persecuted without cause; help me!
Ps 119:128	Truly I direct my steps by *all your precepts*; I hate every false way.
Ps 119:151	Yet you are near, O LORD, and *all your commandments are true*.
Ps 119:160	*The sum of your word* is truth; and *every one of your righteous ordinances* endures forever.
Ps 119:172	My tongue will sing of your promise, for *all your commandments are right*.
Prov 8:8	*All the words of my mouth* are righteous; there is nothing twisted or crooked in them.
Prov 30:5	*Every* word of God proves true; he is a shield to those who take refuge in him.

The Latter Prophets

Jer 11:3–4; cf. v. 8	Thus says the LORD, the God of Israel: Cursed be anyone who does not heed the words of this covenant, which I commanded your ancestors when I brought them out of the land of Egypt, from the iron-smelter, saying, Listen to my voice, and *do all that I command you*. So shall you be my people, and I will be your God . . .
Jer 25:13	I will bring upon that land *all the words that I have uttered against it, everything written in this book*, which Jeremiah prophesied against all the nations.
Jer 26:1, 12	". . . speak to them *all the words* that I command you; *do not hold back a word.*" . . . "It is the LORD who sent me to prophesy against this house and this city *all the words* you have heard."
Jer 30:1	"Write in a book *all the words that I have spoken to you.*"
Jer 36:2; see also vv. 4, 11, 13, 16, 20, 32	"Take a scroll and write on it *all the words that I have spoken to you* against Israel and Judah and all the nations, from the day I spoke to you, from the days of Josiah until today."
Jer 50:21	"go up against [Merathaim]; . . . *do all that I have commanded you.*"
Ezek 3:10	He said to me: Mortal, *all my words that I shall speak to you* receive in your heart and hear with your ears . . .
Ezek 12:23	Tell them therefore, "Thus says the Lord GOD: I will put an end to this proverb, and they shall use it no more as a proverb in Israel." But say to them, The days are near, and *the fulfillment of every vision.*
Ezek 18:19, 21	Yet you say, "Why should not the son suffer for the iniquity of the father?" When the son has done what is lawful and right, and has been *careful to observe all my statutes*, he shall surely live. . . . But if the wicked turn away from all their sins that they have committed and *keep all my statutes* and do what is lawful and right, they shall surely live; they shall not die.
Ezek 40:4	The man said to me, "Mortal, look closely and listen attentively, and set your mind upon *all that I shall show you*, for you were brought here in order that I might show it to you; declare *all that you see* to the house of Israel."
Ezek 44:5	The LORD said to me: Mortal, mark well, look closely, and listen attentively to *all that I shall tell you concerning all the ordinances of the temple of the LORD and all its laws*; and mark well those who may be admitted to the temple and all those who are to be excluded from the sanctuary.

The Annunciation

Luke 2:19	But *Mary treasured all these words* and pondered them in her heart.

The Apocalypse

Rev 1:3	Blessed is the one *who reads aloud the words of the prophecy,* and *blessed are those who hear and who keep what is written in it*; for the time is near.
Rev 22:18–19	I warn everyone who hears *the words of the prophecy of this book: if anyone adds to them, God will add to that person the plagues described in this book; if anyone takes away from the words of the book of this prophecy, God will take away that person's share in the tree of life and in the holy city*, which are described in this book.

CONCLUSION

Although preachers often appeal to "the whole counsel of God" in support of every topic, theme, or public issue under the sun,[25] a more proper understanding of this principle is that we comprehend it comprehensively, so to speak. It is not that the whole counsel of God warrants preaching on every topic,[26] but as Scripture is the written Word of God, it certainly warrants consideration in its fullness in light of the fact that every text is potentially revelatory and bears with it the possibility of transformation. No, it is not every worldly situation that may presume or prevail upon the whole counsel of God; rather, the Word has its own way in the world, on its own terms.

As it is with the "perfect gift" and "perfect law . . . of liberty" (Jas 1:17, 25), so it is with "perfection in love" (1 John 4:18). When Jesus said, "Be perfect [*teleioi*], therefore, as your heavenly Father is perfect [*teleios*]" (Matt 5:48), he was speaking of perfection in love (5:43–48), and doing so with reference to his coming to fulfill the law and the prophets (5:17–20; cf. Rom 13:10). He was, in effect, summoning his disciples to grow into the fullness of love within the framework of a

---

25. See, e.g., Van Ens, "Fearful Preachers Don't Fire at the War Elephant," where the "whole counsel of God" entails a scriptural warrant for preaching sermons against the war in Iraq.

26. As Ronald Allen aptly states, "every noise the world makes is not a call for the church to rethink its practice"; see Allen, *Interpreting the Gospel*, 23.

personal knowledge of and covenantal relationship with God, the fullness of love that corresponds to his own teleological perfection, "to maturity, to the measure of the full stature of Christ" (Eph 4:13). This is the theme of the Epistle of James as well, which asserts that "in fulfillment of his own purpose he gave us birth by the word of truth" (1:18), and urges the saints: "whenever you face trials of any kind, consider it nothing but joy, because you know that the testing of your faith produces endurance; and let endurance have its full effect, so that you may be mature and complete, lacking in nothing" (1:2–4).

How can we even begin to aspire to such perfection unless the entire story of God's love is told, the story of the love of the God who is "holy love"[27] and who loved us first (1 John 4:19), the God without whose prior love we cannot even make a beginning in matters of love, much less hope to reach perfection in love? In short, should not those who truly love God have a hunger to know everything they can possibly learn about him? Should the bride of Christ not long to know everything the Word has revealed of himself? To desire any less does not speak well of the love of the church for her bridegroom. But to pore over and pray over, to study and exegete, to search and learn from and preach the texts that constitute Year D affords the friends and lovers of God a precious opportunity to make a fresh resolution and take a major leap of both faith and love in the right direction.

---

27. "Faith is not ethic, but it is nothing if not ethical. We could not have faith even in infinite love were it not holy love." Forsyth, *Positive Preaching and Modern Mind*, 189. According to Forsyth, judgment is an essential factor in God's revelation of holy love, yet (Forsyth lamented in 1907) this fact is no longer preached.

—4—

The Composition of Year D

YEAR D CONSISTS ALMOST ENTIRELY OF TEXTS HERETOFORE EXCLUDED
from the *RCL*, and as such, is designed to be as objective as possible, even
in the choice of Old Testament texts where a far greater degree of latitude
has been exercised in the selection of texts (and where a great many additional options are proposed). Where it does, for the sake of contextual
clarity, incorporate certain texts already included in Years A, B, and C,
these verses are indicated in parentheses. This bracketing of material,
however, is not intended to suggest that the parenthetical verses are of
minor importance, but simply to signal which verses already receive a
regular voicing in the three-year cycle.

Furthermore, Year D derives its basic shape, as does the *RCL*, from
the two primary foci of the liturgical year (incarnation and resurrection),
so as to complement a three-year cycle or facilitate a four-year cycle
without major disruption, or to simply supplement the *RCL* on a weekly,
Sunday-by-Sunday basis (see Appendix C).

Nevertheless, Year D is peculiar in that it is more radically oriented
toward continuous reading and inclusive selection than it is governed or
"tyrannized" (Sanders) by the calendar. The gospel readings at Christmas
and Easter are not nativity narratives and resurrection appearances *per se*
(since such material is thoroughly represented in the three-year cycle).
Rather, the gospel lections on these high holy days and seasons view
incarnation and resurrection from fresh angles and with new lighting,
so to speak, so as to reframe these events and "redescribe the world"
(Brueggemann) accordingly.

Obviously, a greater degree of latitude has been used in the selection of Old Testament texts, simply because of the vast amount of material available. Yet even here, actual connections (etymological, idiomatic, literary, typological, etc.) and extant arteries of traditional interpretation have been given preference, as have some texts that may, in some cases, invite reinterpretation with the aim of clarifying and purifying the doctrine of the church.

˙ In keeping with certain, but not all, aims of canonical criticism, the goal has been to "interpret the canon holistically," to avoid as far as possible "the notion of a canon within the canon," and to urge "the preacher to interpret voices in the canon that he or she may instinctively reject."[1] As a result, the "poetics of canon" may occasionally outweigh historical-critical assumptions, and typology may play a greater role than it does in the *RCL*, though the aim has been to balance, rather than adjudicate between, competing schools or communities of interpretation suggested by certain "strands" within the fabric of the text.

THE ADVENT–CHRISTMAS–EPIPHANY CYCLE

ADVENT

The design of the Sundays in Advent illustrate to a large degree the approach taken throughout the whole year. While the notion of a "controlling text" as such has not played a dominant role in the composition of Year D, the sequence of selection is certainly significant. The choice of Advent texts began with a consideration of the Gospels and the simple fact that very little gospel material concerning the birth of Christ remains unused. The unused material is either genealogical (Matt 1:1–7; Luke 3:23–38), prologue (Luke 1:1–4), or pertains to the conception, the naming, and the ministry of John the Baptizer (Luke 1:5–25; 1:57–80; 3:19–20); the naming of John by Zechariah, with the miraculous restoration of his speech, includes the famous Song of Zechariah (1:67–80), which finds use as a sung response in Advent, but is not normally taken as a reading or the basis for the sermon. This gospel material, however, can only be distributed over the first three Sundays without protracting things unduly: the Lukan prologue and the promise of the precursor (1:1–25); the naming of John and the Song of Zechariah (1:57–80); and the genealogy (3:22–38 or Matt 1:1–17); thus, it seems appropriate to include material

1. Dozeman, "Canonical Criticism," 15–17.

from the Gospel of John, which (as has been widely noted) is the only Gospel without its own year in the *RCL*, despite its unique theological perspective. Since John lacks nativity material, the first canonical occurrence of unused Johannine material was identified and searched for some angle on the origins of the Christ, and sure enough, the first Johannine lacuna in the *RCL* (John 3:31–38) reads: "The one who comes from above is above all . . . The one who comes from heaven is above all. . . . He whom God has sent speaks the words of God, for he gives the Spirit without measure" (vv. 31 and 34). The larger passage is significant as well for the sense in which it places John's ministry in proper relation to that of Jesus. John declares his role as forerunner openly: he is not the Christ, and he will decrease so that the bridegroom may increase (3:25–30).

As a further counterbalance to Luke's focus on the Baptizer, but in keeping with Luke's priestly themes, it seemed fitting for the epistle reading to commence a semicontinuous sequence of excluded passages from Hebrews, where the High Priesthood of Jesus, as the Son of God, is discussed at length. As mentioned previously, the first epistle reading in Advent sets the tone for Year D by calling for "greater attention to what we have heard, so that we do not drift away from it" (2:1). Owing to the length of the letter and the vast amount of material that has been excluded from the *RCL*, this sequence includes the Sundays of Advent and Christmas and extends through the Fifth Sunday of Ordinary Time (after Epiphany), with the option of concluding the series on Transfiguration, if it preempts the Fourth or Fifth Sundays of Ordinary Time. As liturgical scholars have long noted, Hebrews not only offers a unique Christological perspective, it is also a major source for developing a proper understanding of worship,[2] a concern voiced in the Old Testament lection for First Advent (Mal 1:1–14). Its dominant theme is that of perseverance in the faith, but (as is the case with much of the *RCL*), the consequences of the alternative are muted and obscured, unless the excluded readings are allowed to supply both the backdrop and additional positive assurances to reinforce and elaborate upon the good news as we have it through the *RCL*'s privileged readings: "the promise of entering his rest is still open" (4:1); "we are confident of better things in your case, things that belong to salvation" (6:9); Jesus Christ "is able for all time to save those who

---

2. The first pages of von Allmen's classic text, *Worship*, are thoroughly punctuated with references to Hebrews. In a more recent contribution, Cherry derives the title and master metaphor of her book from Heb 3:3–4. See Cherry, *Worship Architect*, xii–xiv.

approach God through him, since he always lives to make intercession for them" (7:25; see First Sunday of Christmas); "he is the mediator of a better covenant, which has been enacted through better promises" (8:6; see Second Sunday of Christmas); etc.

The Psalm was selected next. In the case of the First and Second Sundays of Advent, Nestle-Aland's *Novum Testamentum Graece* identified multiple references in the Song of Zechariah (Luke 1:67–80) to Psalms 18 and 106, which are either entirely or largely excluded from the *RCL*.

Luke	Psalms
Blessed be the Lord God of Israel, for he has looked favorably on his people and redeemed them. (1:68)	Blessed be the LORD, the God of Israel, from everlasting to everlasting. And let all the people say, "Amen." Praise the LORD! (106:48)
He has raised up a mighty savior for us in the house of his servant David . . . (1:69)	The LORD is my rock, my fortress, and my deliverer, my God, my rock in whom I take refuge, my shield, and the horn of my salvation, my stronghold. I call upon the LORD, who is worthy to be praised; so I shall be saved from my enemies. (18:2–3)
. . . that we would be saved from our enemies and from the hand of all who hate us. (1:71)	He delivered me from my strong enemy, and from those who hated me; for they were too mighty for me. (18:17) So he saved them from the hand of the foe, and delivered them from the hand of the enemy. (106:10)
Thus he has shown the mercy promised to our ancestors, and has remembered his holy covenant . . . (1:72)	For their sake he remembered his covenant, and showed compassion according to the abundance of his steadfast love. (106:45)

Although no such allusions figure in the prologue or the narrative of the annunciation of Gabriel to Zechariah (Luke 1:1–25), the climax of that narrative in Zechariah's song is certainly of a piece with it. Thus, a pairing of these excluded psalms with the Lukan narrative seemed appropriate for the first two Sundays of Advent.

Where the Third Sunday is concerned, the psalm selection has proven more difficult. For though Psalm 95 is prominent in the background of the epistle, it is also heard from twice in Year A of the *RCL*. By contrast, Psalm 81, altogether absent from Nestle-Aland's list of Old Testament citations and allusions, nevertheless speaks of God's liberation of Israel from the toil of slavery and warns the people not to go astray after false gods (Ps 81:6, 9). Similarly, as the epistle makes plain in its interpretation of Psalm 95, the people's hearts go astray (95:10), while the promise of entering God's rest is at stake (95:11). Owing to the similar themes in both Psalms 95 and 81, then, the latter affords a complementary reading and a fresh perspective, especially when we consider that vv. 2–9 of Psalm 81 occur only in the elusive Ninth Sunday of Ordinary Time [Proper 4] (Year B), which rarely occurs.

Psalm 144, selected for the Fourth Sunday of Advent, bears a close relationship to Psalm 18 (cf. 144:5–8 and 18:6–17) and several other psalms (8:4; 90:5–6; and 65:9–13). Here it is loosely paired with the gospel by virtue of its status as a royal Davidic psalm and the messianic, nuptial overtones in the gospel lection. Otherwise, the lections for this Fourth Sunday serve to contrast (as do many Year D texts) warnings of wrath for those who fall away or turn back from following the LORD, with assurances of blessing and prosperity for those who hold fast to the promises God has sworn to fulfill and the hope that has appeared in Jesus Christ.

The Old Testament selections were the last to be made, not just in Advent but throughout Year D. While the gospel lection for First Advent alludes to Mal 3:1, this text already occurs in the *RCL*. Nevertheless, strong associations persist between Malachi's anticipation of Elijah's return (Mal 4:5–6)—both prophets being reformers of worship (Mal 1:1–14; 1 Kings 18)—and the typological correlations that the gospels reveal between Elijah and the Baptizer. Thus, a similarly provocative and dialectical reading from Malachi (1:1–14) is proposed, one that, despite its painful, pointed rhetoric (1:1–5), absolutely must be read theologically, not through the lens of superimposed anthropological, nationalistic, or ethnic categories: it is not about *foreigners*, but *foreign gods* (2:11). More to the point is the question posed by the prophet regarding the sincerity of worship: "If then I am a father, where is the honor due to me?" (1:6–14). Malachi's oracle is a summons, couched in the form of a series of questions and rebukes, to return to the LORD's altar wholeheartedly and with pure offerings.

The selection of Numbers 12 for Second Advent is based on the fact that the epistle (Heb 3:2, 5) twice quotes Num 12:7 in establishing both Moses' credentials and Jesus' superiority. The chapter itself recounts the criticisms made of Moses by Aaron and Miriam for his interracial marriage and Miriam's temporary punishment (a bout of leprosy). Numbers 20 is suggested as an alternative, where we read of Moses' own failure to show the LORD's holiness in the incident at Meribah (20:1–13), for which he was not permitted to enter the promised land. The chapter includes the account of Aaron's death (20:22–29), with a reminder of Aaron's part in the rebellion at Meribah (v. 24). Each of the instances contrasts the fallibility of these Old Testament saints with the sinless perfection of Jesus, in keeping with the thrust of the epistle (Heb 3:1–19).

A pairing of Josh 23:1–16 with the epistle for Fourth Advent (Heb 5:11—6:20) would have been more direct, due to their parallel warnings against apostasy (cf. Josh 23:16 and Heb 6:4–6). As it is, Joshua's farewell discourse, similar to but distinct from the more famous Shechem covenant (Josh 24), has been selected for Third Advent so as to place it in conversation with the epistle (Heb 4:1–11) and the psalms (81 and 95), all of which are concerned, in one way or another—spatially, geographically, temporally, and eternally—with the prospect of entering and remaining in God's "rest."

Finally, the choice of Numbers 14 for Fourth Advent might also have been paired directly with the epistle for Second Advent (Heb 3:1–19) by virtue of no less than three citations and allusions (cf. Num 14:21–23, 29, 32; and Heb 3:11, 17, 18), but such repetition is already evident in the epistle. As it is, Num 14:1–25 has been chosen for Fourth Advent so as to recall the intergenerational consequences of Israel's refusal to enter the promised land when first instructed to do so, to uphold the faithful examples of certain individuals (Joshua and Caleb), and to juxtapose this incident of rebellion with the epistle, where the curse of apostasy is contrasted with the doubly unchangeable assurances of God's oath to fulfill his promises to those who hope in the priestly ministry of Jesus Christ, himself "a sure and steadfast anchor of the soul" (Heb 6:19).

CHRISTMAS

Not surprisingly, apart from the gospel lections already chosen for Advent, no further nativity narratives lie undiscovered or unused (this side of extracanonical gnosticism and heterodoxy) by the *RCL*. Thus, the gospel selections for Christmas (Propers I, II, and III) and the two Sundays of Christmas have proven most difficult. Indeed, they may at first appear the most unsatisfactory and challenging in Year D. One can scarcely imagine *not* making use of the traditional infancy narratives in Matthew and Luke, and for the record, the fact that they are not included in Year D does not mean that they should be omitted from Christmas services altogether. The experimental approach taken here, however, is simply to ask: What would these gospel texts (Matt 8:14–34; 10:9–23; 11:1–30; 12:22–50; Mark 5:1–20; Luke 7:18–35; 11:14–54; 12:1–12; and John 12:17–19, 37–50), taken from the ministry and teaching of Jesus, sound like at Christmas? In many cases, the irony is heightened by virtue of the occasion.

> ". . . the Son of Man has nowhere to lay his head." (Matt 8:20)

> "What sort of man is this, that even the winds and the sea obey him?" (Matt 8:27)

> Then the whole town came out to meet Jesus; and when they saw him, they begged him to leave their neighborhood. (Matt 8:34)

> "See, I am sending you out like sheep into the midst of wolves; so be wise as serpents and innocent as doves." (Matt 10:16)

> ". . . the Son of Man came eating and drinking, and they say, 'Look, a glutton and a drunkard, a friend of tax collectors and sinners!' Yet wisdom is vindicated by her deeds." (Matt 11:19)

> "I thank you, Father, Lord of heaven and earth, because you have hidden these things from the wise and the intelligent and have revealed them to infants; yes, Father, for such was your gracious will." (Matt 11:25–26)

> ". . . how can one enter a strong man's house and plunder his property, without first tying up the strong man? Then indeed the house can be plundered. Whoever is not with me is against me, and whoever does not gather with me scatters." (Matt 12:29–30)

> "The good person brings good things out of a good treasure, and the evil person brings evil things out of an evil treasure. I tell you, on the day of judgment you will have to give an account for every careless word you utter." (Matt 12:35–36)

"Who is my mother, and who are my brothers?" And pointing to his disciples, he said, "Here are my mother and my brothers! For whoever does the will of my Father in heaven is my brother and sister and mother." (Matt 12:49–50)

While he was saying this, a woman in the crowd raised her voice and said to him, "Blessed is the womb that bore you and the breasts that nursed you!" But he said, "Blessed rather are those who hear the word of God and obey it!" (Luke 11:27–28)

"Your eye is the lamp of your body. If your eye is healthy, your whole body is full of light; but if it is not healthy, your body is full of darkness. Therefore consider whether the light in you is not darkness. If then your whole body is full of light, with no part of it in darkness, it will be as full of light as when a lamp gives you light with its rays." (Luke 11:34–36)

Most of these texts will be recognizable as unused synoptic parallels of texts that are used in the *RCL*, and in many cases the variation between synoptic sources is relatively inconsequential. One clearly unparalleled text is the Johannine reading chosen for Christmas Day as well as Christ the King Sunday (12:17–19, 37–50). There we read, among other things:

The Pharisees then said to one another, "You see, you can do nothing. Look, the world has gone after him!" (12:19)

Although he had performed so many signs in their presence, they did not believe in him. (12:37)

Nevertheless many, even of the authorities, believed in him. But because of the Pharisees they did not confess it, for fear that they would be put out of the synagogue; they loved human glory more than the glory that comes from God. (12:42–43)

"Whoever believes in me believes not in me but in him who sent me. And whoever sees me sees him who sent me. I have come as light into the world, so that everyone who believes in me should not remain in the darkness. I do not judge anyone who hears my words and does not keep them, for I came not to judge the world, but to save the world. The one who rejects me and does not receive my word has a judge; on the last day the word that I have spoken will serve as judge, for I have not spoken on my own, but the Father who sent me has himself given me a commandment about what to say and what to speak. And I know that

his commandment is eternal life. What I speak, therefore, I speak
just as the Father has told me." (12:44–50)

As with many other Johannine texts, one wonders in amazement that
such a passage as this—"I came not to judge the world, but to save"; "his
commandment is eternal life!"—has been excluded from the *RCL*. Reading
this passage at Christmas, with its light/darkness motif and the strong iden-
tification between the sending Father and the Son who is sent with saving
purpose, offers rich material for interpretation of the incarnation and a
fresh approach to the *missio Dei*.

The epistle lessons for the Sundays of Christmas track the semicontinuous reading of Hebrews, as previously mentioned. For the Christmas
Propers (I–III), selections from James and Romans are suggested. Although
Jas 1:17–27 occurs once in Year B (22nd Ordinary/Proper 17), the occasion of Christmas Eve seems a fitting time to reconsider the "straw epistle"
(Luther) in light of its subtle Christological imagery, especially its references to the new "birth by the word of truth," to "every generous act of
giving, with every perfect gift . . . from above, coming down from the Father
of lights," and to the meek reception of "the implanted word that has the
power to save your souls" (Jas 1:17–21).

In addition, two selections from Romans are suggested for Christmas
Morning and Christmas Day. The first contains an excluded passage of
monumental importance: "But now, apart from law, the righteousness of
God has been disclosed, and is attested by the law and the prophets, the
righteousness of God through faith in Jesus Christ for all who believe"
(Rom 3:21–22a). The latter offers (as noted in chapter 2) one of "the most
'inclusive' visions in all the Bible" (Rutledge), as it speaks of both "the full
number of the Gentiles" (11:25) entering the kingdom, and the "full inclusion" of the Jews (11:12), so that "all Israel will be saved" (11:26). As with
the alternative and seemingly tangential gospel passages, the opportunity
is ripe for shedding new light on the *missio Dei*, to shift from narrative
accounts of *how* Jesus came, to more teleological considerations of *why* he
came and what he has promised to do when he returns.[3]

---

3. This is in keeping with the origins of Christmas in the earlier festival of Epiphany,
which, as White has written, is "older than Christmas and has a deeper meaning. For
instead of simply being an anniversary of the birth of Christ, it testifies to the whole purpose of the incarnation: the manifestation of God in Jesus Christ, beginning both with
his birth and with the beginning of his ministry (the baptism when he is proclaimed, 'My
Son, the Beloved'). And the mighty signs and teachings, narrated in the Gospel as Jesus

The psalms selected for the Christmas season are Psalms 21, 44, 35, 94, 110, and 73. The royal coronation Psalm 21 (Christmas Eve) celebrates the king's trust in the LORD and the LORD's eternal blessing and defense of the king; both exultant (vv. 1–7) and apocalyptic (vv. 8–12), this psalm speaks of the relationship between king and LORD with such intimacy and fluidity in its use of pronouns, the two appear virtually indistinguishable, as is befitting a psalm to be read or sung at the Feast of the Incarnation.

Psalm 44 (Christmas Morning) is a communal lament, sung by a people oppressed and disheartened at their sense that God has abandoned them in battle. Yet they remind the LORD of his covenant, claim they have kept it faithfully, and declare they have not turned back from following him. The psalmist expresses incredulity at the fact that God appears to be asleep:

> Rouse yourself! Why do you sleep, O Lord? . . .
> Why do you hide your face? . . .
> Rise up, come to our help.
> Redeem us for the sake of your steadfast love. (Ps 44:23, 24, 26)

As with many other Christmas lections, the occasion lends this desperate plea an unmistakable ring of poignant irony, with Immanuel in our midst, humble and hidden in plain sight, embarking on a mission of not merely national but cosmic redemption.

Two psalms are suggested for Christmas Day, neither of which is afforded a hearing in the *RCL*, but both of which bear some relation to the epistle (Rom 11:2b–36). Both are difficult psalms of lament. Psalm 35 is an individual plea to the LORD for protection. Though the psalmist asks for "ruin" for his traitorous enemies, the greater emphasis is on the psalmist's need for deliverance, rescue, and the vindication of his blamelessness and good intentions in interceding for those who now persecute him. Furthermore, it appeals to God on the grounds that divine intervention will bring thanksgiving and enhance the glory of the LORD's reputation. In short, it is a "glorious" psalm that, despite its splenetic moments, is no more vengeful than the popular Magnificat (Luke 1:46–55).

Similarly, Psalm 94 is a communal lament that, despite its startling way of addressing the LORD as "you God of vengeance" (94:1) and its

---

accomplished this manifestation, provide an opportunity in the Season after Epiphany (or Ordinary Time) for commemoration of those works and teachings of Jesus that led up to the final events in Jerusalem." White, *Introduction to Christian Worship*, 62.

certainty that that the LORD will obliterate the wicked (94:23), is nevertheless cited in the epistle so as to reassure the reader that God has "by no means" rejected his people Israel (cf. Rom 11:1–2 and Ps 94:14).

Several things should be remembered when praying such psalms:

1. They are best understood and allowed to stand as songs of the Holy Spirit,[4] or the prayers of the messianic king himself, and as such should be offered in the name of Jesus Christ our intercessor, who knows best how to interpret and apply them.[5]

2. From a New Testament perspective, the enemies in the psalms are "not . . . enemies of flesh and blood," but "the spiritual forces of evil in the heavenly places" (Eph 6:10–17), the "principalities" and "powers" in service of the arch enemy or "the ruler of the power of the air" (2:1–2).[6]

3. Existentially speaking, the "destruction" of an enemy need not entail the clinical death of a person, but may well amount to (and is best interpreted as) their conversion: dying and rising with Christ.

4. Finally, the full canon of Scripture—our charitable, mitigating interpretations notwithstanding—undeniably speaks of an ultimate, final judgment, and this judgment is brought about not so much by the "verdict" or "vengeance" of the divine judge, but by the very reality of his holy presence. This is true of the incarnation as well as the crucifixion of Jesus, but we must also admit of this certainty when we consider those apocalyptic prophecies that speak of "the man of lawlessness" being destroyed by the very breath of the returning Christ, "by the manifestation of his coming" (2 Thess 2:1–12).

Much as the preacher should ever seek for the gracious, hopeful interpretation, the "good news" in these difficult texts, there comes a point at which our text selection and preaching must frankly acknowledge these undeniable realities such that the culmination of Scripture itself resounds

4. Old, *Worship*, 43–44.

5. Holladay urges that the psalms should be offered in prayer "through Jesus Christ our Lord," since Jesus Christ is the only one who can *safely* pray the psalms when they condemn the enemies of God; "only for (Jesus Christ) was evil completely external." The phrase "through Jesus Christ our Lord" means he is "both the mediator and the censor of our prayers: he sponsors our prayers, but what is unworthy of him we are asking him to block." See Holladay, *Psalms through Three Thousand Years*, 311–13, 345–58, esp. 348.

6. Ibid., 351–58.

with this sigh of lament and resignation: "Let the evildoer still do evil, and the filthy still be filthy, and the righteous still do right, and the holy still be holy" (Rev 22:11). That is a fearsome word to read aloud, a terrible and sobering resignation, but it is a word that the wise, in whom wisdom and the fear of the LORD have made a beginning, will not fail to acknowledge.

These same considerations apply to Psalm 110, which is cited in the New Testament more often than any other psalm (over two dozen times), and while many of these quotations and allusions make their way into the *RCL*, many others do not. Furthermore, these New Testament references focus on only three of its seven verses (110:1, 4, and 5); meanwhile, the *RCL* never once provides for this brief royal psalm to be read in its entirety. Here, Year D assigns this important psalm to the First Sunday of Christmas, when the epistle (Heb 7:1–18), in an extended exposition of this very psalm and the Old Testament lection (Gen 14:1–24), compares and contrasts the Levitical priesthood with the order of Melchizedek. (Indeed, in Year D, First Christmas should perhaps be known as Melchizedek Sunday.)

As noted in chapter 1, Brueggemann describes Psalm 73 as one of the "most satisfying" psalms in the canon, no doubt for the therapeutic fact that it allows the plaintive psalmist to fully vent his protest against the prosperity of the wicked, and ends with a spirit of sobriety, of "coming to" with gratitude for God's guidance and protection, and for the hope of eternity in the LORD's presence. While this psalm bears no direct literary relation to the other lections for the Second Sunday of Christmas, it certainly hinges on the same qualitative difference between heaven and earth that we see in the epistle (Heb 8:1–13), where the Mosaic tabernacle (Exod 25:1–40) and the heavenly sanctuary are contrasted.

The Old Testament readings for Christmas present a variety of options. Two texts from Ecclesiastes (5:1–20 or 7:1–14) are suggested for Christmas Eve, along with a reading from Ezekiel (33:23–33), each of which serves to refine the reader's understanding of what makes for proper worship, especially on Christmas Eve: holy fear and silence, a quickness to listen, and a care with words in the house of God (Eccl 5:1–7); recognition that earthly existence is more a time for mourning and tears than the loud, vain laughter of fools and that, particularly where the mission of Christ is concerned, "the end of a thing [is better] than its beginning" (Eccl 7:1–8); and finally, that songs that are merely beautiful and the poetic oracles of the prophets are not to be compared (Ezek

33:30–32). Other shared themes, such as warnings against rashness and anger, will also be evident (cf. Eccl 7:9 and Jas 1:19–20), while warnings against indulgent nostalgia (Eccl 7:10) may be particularly needful on Christmas Eve.

The balance of Ecclesiastes 7 (vv. 15–29) is suggested for Christmas Morning, not simply for the possibility of a more thorough, continuous reading of this wisdom chapter, but for its declaration of the universality of sin: "Surely there is no one on earth so righteous as to do good without ever sinning" (Eccl 7:20), a sentiment echoed elsewhere in this chapter (7:21, 29, et al.), and given prominence in the epistle (Rom 3:20). Micah 7:1–20 likewise describes the depraved human condition in sweeping, inclusive terms; yet over the course of the oracle, the humbling of the nations is assured (7:15–17), and God, who "delights in showing clemency," is exalted for his ultimately gracious, forgiving nature (7:18–20). Again, if the question we bring to these readings is missional and teleological, concerned with *why* Christ came, we will find rich material for proclamation from these overlooked prophetic and wisdom texts.

On Christmas Day, the Old Testament options include the bewildering message given to Isaiah to proclaim after his call, namely, that the recipients of the word will be unable to perceive it (6:9–13), and the word of Jeremiah regarding the senselessness of idols and the stupidity of those who worship them (10:1–25). As often as the former is mentioned in the New Testament, the *RCL* takes pains to avoid it. Rather than glossing over this troublesome theme of stupidity and senselessness, however, Christmas is a wonderful occasion for addressing the dialectic of God's revelation and hiddenness (*á la* Barth) head on.[7] The epistle (Rom 11:8), quoting Isa 29:10, and the gospel (John 12:17–19), beg the question: Why is it that those who should have been the first to recognize Jesus did not, could not, would not, or have not (yet) done so?

As has been suggested, the Old Testament lections (Genesis 14 and Exodus 25) for the Sundays of Christmas take their cue from the sequential epistle reading of Hebrews. In a return to the sort of typological pairing that the *RCL* shunned, the readings for these Sundays are those that stand most clearly in the background of the apostle's interpretation of the mysterious Melchizedek (First Christmas) and the temporary purpose of the Mosaic tabernacle (Second Christmas).

---

7. Slemmons, *Groans of the Spirit*, xvi–xvii, 4–11, 40–44, et al.

Epiphany (January 6)

Perhaps the most important Johannine texts retrieved in Year D are found in John 5 and 12. While John 5:19–30 is given the highest place of prominence on Resurrection/Easter Day, John 5:31–47 and 12:1–19, 37–50 are given two occasions, one Sunday and one fixed feast day. While the missing verses of John 12 are assigned to Christmas and Christ the King Sunday, the culmination of John 5 is assigned to both the 13th Sunday of Ordinary Time and Epiphany (January 6). Here the focus is on multiple witnesses to Jesus, from human prophets Moses (5:45–47) and John (5:31–35), to the miracles of Jesus (5:36) and the inspired Scriptures that "testify on [his] behalf" (5:39–40), to the Father himself (5:37–38). Jesus, however, downplays the acceptability of human testimony, while clearly upholding the divine, even nascently Trinitarian, witnesses that validate his testimony to himself (5:31).

This gospel text is paired with an important and essential but overlooked chapter from the Johannine epistles, the disuse and neglect of which has proven extremely dangerous and costly in recent decades. First John 2:3–29 is accorded three opportunities to speak in Year D: at Epiphany, Ascension, and on 18th Ordinary. This seemingly dichotomous chapter, bracing as it is, delineates clearly between (1) obedient disciples who are known by love, and "liars" who hate their brothers and sisters and abide in darkness; (2) the love of the Father and the love of the world, which are here shown to be mutually exclusive; and (3) the anointed knowledge of the truth, and the deceiving spirit of the antichrist that denies the messianic identity of Jesus. This text is every bit as important for cultivating the gift of spiritual discernment as that other excluded Johannine text, 1 John 4:1–6, where we are urged to "test the spirits to see whether they are from God" (v. 1), by which "we know the spirit of truth and the spirit of error" (v. 6; see Tenth Ordinary). These Johannine texts, simplistic though they may at first seem, are highly epiphanic and illuminating; it is fitting, and perhaps providential, that they follow the more puzzling Christmas selections from the prophets that attest to a lack of discernment among, even the stupidity of, those who look for God in all the wrong places.

Psalms 75 and 76 serve as options for Epiphany, Resurrection Day, or Resurrection Evening. One a national thanksgiving (Psalm 75), the other a Song of Zion (Ps 76), both psalms celebrate the victory of God over the nations, "putting down one and lifting up another" (75:7), rising up "to establish judgment, to save all the oppressed of the earth" (76:9). God's "wonderful deeds" are the subject of testimony and cause for the psalmist to sing, "I will rejoice forever" (75:9), and to tell "all who are around" the LORD to "bring gifts to the one who is awesome" (76:11).

One of the most important Old Testament lections in Year D occurs here, as well as on 17th Ordinary, for if the Great Commandment (Deut 6:4–6) summarizes the law (Deut 5:6–21), then Deuteronomy 4:9–40 contextualizes it, both the giving of the law (4:9–31) and the unprecedented deliverance of Israel by the LORD, which sets God's reputation far and away above any other god and his saving acts completely apart from what other "gods" have attempted (4:32–40). The Deuteronomistic theme—the LORD's superiority in the contest between the gods (though it is never a contest among equals)—is arguably so important that it normalizes interpretation of everything from Exodus (in retrospect) through the Deuteronomistic History (going forward); its covenantal terms anticipate the exile itself (as do other Deuteronomic texts), while the theme of divine contest is eventually taken up in the restoration prophesies of Isaiah and in the cultural (or better yet, theological) fastidiousness of the reformer Nehemiah.

BAPTISM OF THE LORD THROUGH TRANSFIGURATION

The gospel accounts of the baptism of the Lord Jesus receive a thorough treatment in the *RCL*. In Year D, the gospel concerns John's death (Matt 14:1–12), while the Old Testament lection details the annual rite of the Day of Atonement (Lev 16:1–34), which is discussed at length in the epistle (Heb 9:1–28) and reframed in light of Christ's entry "into heaven itself." Perhaps the most baptismal, or at least watery, lection is Psalm 69, which opens with the cry, "Save me, O God, for the waters have come up to my neck" (69:1); but the death of the Baptizer, the Levitical instructions to a bereaved and sullen Aaron (after the death of his sons Nadab and Abihu for offering unholy fire before the LORD), and the description of the heavenly scene in which Jesus, "with his own blood, . . . offered himself without blemish to God to purify our conscience from dead works to worship the living God" (Heb 9:11–14), together afford a marvelous opportunity to view the baptism of Christ in panoramic, even epiphanic and eschatological perspective (9:28). For the scene in the Jordan itself, if it monopolizes the occasion, has a drastically reductive and oversimplifying effect, especially when Jesus himself declares, well *after* his baptism by John, that his baptism remains incomplete (Luke 12:50) until he has been to the cross (John 19:30).

The epistle sequence for the Sundays following the Baptism of the Lord completes the semicontinuous course through Hebrews, then turns to 2 Peter for three Sundays (6th through 8th Ordinary) and Jude (Transfiguration); the preacher is encouraged, however, to bring Hebrews to an orderly conclusion in anticipation of the fact that Ordinary Time is often interrupted prematurely, sometimes as early as 4th Ordinary, with Quinquagesima (the Sunday before Ash Wednesday or the Seventh Sunday before Easter), as it was once called. The prospect of such an interruption may not be entirely unwelcome, of course, as these letters, in addition to exhorting the saints to holiness (2 Pet 1:1–21; Jude 20–22), contain strident denouncements of false teachers and apostates (2 Pet 2:1—3:7; Jude 4–13) and apocalyptic prophecies regarding "the last days" (3:1–7; Jude 14–19) and "the day of the Lord (2 Pet 3:8–13). Nevertheless, the final word is one of peace and patience: the saints are to "strive to be found at peace," and take comfort in the salvific patience of the Lord (3:15), who does "not [want] any to perish, but all to come to repentance" (3:9).

The gospel readings for 2nd–4th Ordinary are alternative synoptic readings of healing miracles that are often more succinct than the versions preferred by the *RCL*. In selecting a particular synoptic parallel, the *RCL* normally favors the longer version, which is only fitting. Thus, while Mark is normally hasty and breathless in style, certain Markan accounts are actually more elaborate than their Matthean and Lukan counterparts. The point here is simply to view familiar events in the early, earthly ministry of Jesus from the perspective of a different evangelist: the healings of a leprous man (Matt 8:1–4; Luke 5:12–16), a paralytic (Matt 9:1–8; Luke 5:17–26), and a man with a withered hand (Matt 12:9–14; Luke 6:6–11); and the calling of the disciples (Mark 3:13–18; Luke 6:12–16).

Oddly enough, owing to the weekly liturgical use of the Lord's Prayer, Matthew's version of the prayer itself (Matt 6:7–15) is never read in the *RCL*. The 5th Sunday of Ordinary Time provides an opportunity for doing so, before turning (for 6th and 7th Ordinary) to the remaining verses of the Sermon on the Mount (7:1–20) that have been excluded from the three-year cycle. These include warnings against judging others with hypocrisy and casting pearls before swine (7:16), and admonitions to be wary of false prophets (7:15–20) and to enter through the narrow gate (7:13–14). On 8th Ordinary, the gospel recounts the rejection of Jesus in his hometown, and on Transfiguration, in the absence of any other gospel accounts of Jesus' metamorphosis, two accounts are proposed that involve Jesus' healing at a distance with a word: in one case, the servant of a centurion who recognizes Jesus' authority (Matt 8:5–13), and in the other, the son of a desperate royal official (John 4:43–54). What does this have to do with *the* transfiguration? Perhaps the question may be better posed in terms of awe, wonder, and authority.

The psalms for this season are diverse, including imprecation (109), a royal fragment (89:5–18, 38–52), individual thanksgiving (34:11–18), individual lament (28), communal lament (12), a Torah psalm (119:1–32), and songs of trust (61 and 11); in most cases these are selected in relation to the epistles, which also guide the Old Testament selection from Isaiah (26:7—27:1) for 2nd Ordinary.

For the remainder of this season (3rd Ordinary through Transfiguration), the Old Testament reading proceeds *lectio continua* through the entire series of speeches by Elihu, the mysterious, vanishing, messianic (or at least anti-Satanic) friend of Job (32–37). This may seem a strangely protracted and exhaustive selection, especially since no other options have been suggested here, but this intense focus is warranted in light of (1) the likelihood that the season will be truncated by Transfiguration; (2) the fact that these chapters do not even appear in the *Daily Lectionary*; and (3) reading them Christologically offers rich insights for understanding the intercessory role of the priestly Messiah as interpreted in Hebrews. The typological similarities between Elihu and Christ are striking and numerous indeed, meriting extended consideration that modern scholarship has largely overlooked or dismissed prematurely.

THE LENT–RESURRECTION–PENTECOST CYCLE

Ash Wednesday, Lent, and Holy Week

In conceiving Year D as a means of mediating (via the objective norm of the canon) between *lectio continua* and *lectio selecta*, the idea of dialectical reading presented itself, not so much with the aim of dialogue for dialogue's sake, but with the hope of clarification.[8] Thus, in many

---

8. See Slemmons, *Groans of the Spirit*, xvii and 36.

respects, this entire proposal may be described as *lectio dialectica*, an approach that (1) includes the excluded voices of Scripture, not in pretense, but in actuality; and (2) aspires to do so thoroughly, even as it admits, practically speaking, that it falls short of this goal, while anticipating future advances toward it.

Meanwhile, two features of the selections in Lent demonstrate in a narrower sense what I mean by *lectio dialectica*. First, the gospel readings from the middle chapters of John, including 5:1–18, but especially 7:1–8:59, involve a series of notoriously difficult exchanges between Jesus and various groups, including his own brothers, and those with differing opinions regarding his identity: the Jews, the crowd, the Pharisees, the chief priests, the temple police, certain elders and scribes, Nicodemus, etc. In the verbal melee, the ambiguity is perhaps thicker than in most gospel passages, including the parables and the passion narratives. Discerning a straightforward claim is not easy, since the dramatic level is so high, and there are so many competing voices to sort out. Jesus' words are as figurative here as anywhere and his actions puzzling, as when, for example, he announces that he is not going to the festival, then goes *in cognito*. In short, the whole scene is typical of the sort of verbal contestation that characterizes *dialectic*. While John employs neither the Greek *dialog-* or *dialeg-*, there is dialogue proper in the purest sense among those "looking for an opportunity to kill him" (7:1), in the complaining and muttering of the crowds (7:12, 20, 32, et al.), in the reactionary attempts of the Pharisees to arrest him (7:30), etc. But there is also dialectic at work, and this is evident in the incipient understanding of the identity of Jesus voiced by others in the crowd, and even by some among the authorities (e.g., Nicodemus). One unavoidable characteristic of this dialectical section, however, is the "division in the crowd because of him" (7:43), what Kierkegaard terms "essential offense": the sense in which the God-man cannot avoid the possibility of giving offense, for he cannot deny himself.[9]

Another dialectical feature designed into the season of Lent involves the epistle readings, specifically, the possibility of alternating omitted lections from Paul (i.e., Galatians) and James, with the aim of refining and clarifying key aspects of New Testament theology, for example, the relation between faith and works. Another option is to simply preach through either of these letters, roughly one chapter at a time, in the mode

9. Kierkegaard, *Practice in Christianity*, 122–44.

of the *Westminster Directory*. But, since real or apparent contradiction is a key characteristic of dialectic, a more purely dialectical reading would intentionally bring contrasting perspectives into the foreground, not so as to demonstrate inconsistency, but with the hope of resolution. Thus, the season of Lent actually provides (at least) three options for the epistle reading: *lectio continua* through either Galatians or James, or a semi-sequential debate between the two. Further provision is also made for such a series to begin either on Ash Wednesday or on First Lent. With the conclusion of either dialectical or continuous readings, omitted verses from Romans 1 and 2, 1 Peter 4, and 1 Corinthians 15 are suggested for the epistle readings in Holy Week (Palm Sunday through the Great Vigil). Before one recoils, however, at the difficult verses from Romans 1, one should bear in mind that these are matched with the leveling, universalizing prohibitions against judging others found in Romans 2.

In Holy Week, the textually problematic gospel passage regarding the woman caught in the act of adultery (John 7:53—8:11) is assigned to Maundy Thursday. This selection is made for largely practical reasons: it is simply the last remaining unused text from the middle chapters of John assigned to Lent, and it continues the confrontational theme that characterizes the gospel readings in this season. On a peculiar note, while we are accustomed to reading of the footwashing on Maundy Thursday (John 13:11–20), Jesus' intervention for the sake of the woman here is the only other scene in which he clearly stoops for the sake of his intercessory intervention. Another option for Maundy Thursday is Luke's unusual account of the Last Supper, which includes unique "red letter" material (22:15, et al.) that Kierkegaard suggested might bear inclusion in the words of institution.[10] Likewise, the Lukan passion narrative assigned to Good Friday includes other unique material (23:31, et al.) that is virtually unknown owing to the present shape of the *RCL*.

In choosing psalms for Lent, the first recourse was to four of the seven "penitential psalms" overlooked by the *RCL*: Psalms 102 (Ash Wednesday), 6 (First Lent), 143 (Second Lent) and 38 (Third Lent).[11] While the two psalms suggested for Palm Sunday (35 and 94) are, owing

10. Kierkegaard, *Christian Discourses*, 251–61.

11. Psalm 143 appears in the *RCL*, but only on the Easter Vigil. That only three of the seven penitential psalms appear on the Sundays in the whole of the *RCL* indicates the lengths to which the designers have gone to downplay penitential themes. But the reader will have gathered by now that repentance is a major theme that Year D seeks to reclaim.

to the royal occasion, identical with those suggested for Christmas Day, the psalms for the remaining Sundays (39 and 101) have strong confessional elements. In Psalm 39, the psalmist is deeply mindful of his own mortality (39:4–6) and prays for deliverance from all of his transgressions (39:8). In Psalm 101, he admits that he has not yet attained to "the way that is blameless" (101:2), but expresses his longing for it, along with his resolution to uphold loyalty, justice, integrity, and to repudiate perverseness of heart, evil, arrogance, and deceit (101:1, 3b–8). He resolves to guard his eyes from the sight of base things (v. 3a)—a worthy goal, especially in the present age. Although Psalm 113 is already used in the *RCL*, it seems appropriate to assign it to Maundy Thursday, in keeping with its use at Passover as the first of the Egyptian Hallel psalms (113–18). For Good Friday, Psalm 88 is suggested; this lament psalm, the plea of a desperate individual, is peculiar for its lack of any discernible "turn" from complaint to praise (a normal feature of most lament psalms). Here, the theme of forsakenness that persists throughout and the dark note of finality seem fitting for this one day of the year, when hope must be deferred and sought somewhere beyond the psalm itself.

The Old Testament readings in Lent unfold between two great penitential prayers of Nehemiah 9 (First Lent) and Ezra 9 (Good Friday). Numerous diverse texts are suggested as well, with particular emphasis on Genesis, Deuteronomy, and especially the prophets. Isaiah sets the tone for revival and healing on Ash Wednesday: "Build up, build up, prepare the way, remove every obstruction from my people's way. . . . I have seen their ways, but I will heal them" (57:1–21). The seminal story of Cain and Abel (Gen 4:1–16) is assigned for Fourth Lent, wherein God tells Cain that "sin is lurking at the door; its desire is for you, but you must master it" (4:7). The separation of Lot from Abram (Genesis 13) is followed by the LORD's promise of a singular "offspring," a promise quoted by Paul in the epistle for Third Lent (Gal 3:16) with which it is paired.

Three texts from Deuteronomy are suggested that reiterate the *Shema'* (11:13) and speak of the LORD's requirement (in more consistently theological terms than does the popular and memorable Mic 6:8), the circumcision of the heart (10:16; 30:6), and the nearness of the Word (30:11–14).

Ezekiel 47:1–12 is paired with the gospel for Second Lent, in which Jesus promises "rivers of living water" (John 7:37–39); David's prayer of thanksgiving for the everlasting covenant (2 Sam 7:18–29) is paired with John 7:42 (Third Lent), where the crowd seeks to understand the Messiah's origins in relation to David.

In addition to the penitential prayer of Ezra 9, other options for Good Friday focus on Jeremiah's vision of the cup of wrath and staggering (25:15–38) and the promise given to Solomon (at the dedication of the temple) that the whole land would be healed if the covenantal people of God repent: "if my people who are called by my name humble themselves, pray, seek my face, and turn from their wicked ways, then I will hear from heaven, and will forgive their sin and heal their land" (2 Chr 7:1–22, esp. v. 14). Otherwise, readings from Isaiah predominate, frequently with Galatians in view:

Ash Wednesday	Isa 57:1–21	"The righteous perish, and no one takes it to heart . . ."
Fourth Lent	Isa 54:1–17 or Isa 37:14–38	"Sing, O barren one who did not bear . . ." or ". . . hear all the words of Sennacherib, which he has sent to mock the living God."
Fifth Lent	Isa 63:(7–9) 10–19	". . . you, O LORD, are our father; our Redeemer from of old is your name."
Sixth Lent/ Palm	Isa 43:8–15	"I, I am the LORD, and besides me there is no savior."

RESURRECTION, PENTECOST, AND TRINITY

In the absence of any unused resurrection appearances of Jesus, the gospel lections for the season of Easter/Resurrection make use of texts in which Jesus speaks of the resurrection, either prophetically or didactically. As mentioned above, the gospel for Resurrection Day is John 5:19–30, wherein Jesus says:

> Indeed, just as the Father raises the dead and gives them life, so also the Son gives life to whomever he wishes. . . . [A]nyone who hears my word and believes him who sent me has eternal life, and does not come under judgment, but has passed from death to life. . . . Very truly, I tell you, the hour is coming, and is now here, when the dead will hear the voice of the Son of God, and those who hear will live. . . . Do not be astonished at this; for the hour is coming when all who are in their graves will hear his voice and will come out—those who have done good, to the resurrection of life, and those who have done evil, to the resurrection of condemnation. (5:21, 24–25, 28–29)

More unique Johannine material is assigned sequentially to 2nd (16:16–24) and 3rd Easter (16:25–33). Here Jesus, in his farewell discourse, promises that although the disciples will experience pain at their separation from him, they will see him again. He also speaks of returning to the Father, promising peace, "complete" joy, and a new level of effective intercession for the disciples; finally, he attests to the pain and persecution they will know in the world, but he assures them, "take courage; I have conquered the world!"

The gospels then turn to synoptic parallels for different perspectives on familiar texts. The gospel assigned to 4th Easter is either the Matthean or Markan account of Jesus' debate with the Sadducees regarding the resurrection (Luke's version occurs in Year C, with a truncated ending). For 5th Easter, the gospel again comes from Matthew or Mark, this time involving the second miraculous feeding (Matt 15:32—16:12; Mark 8:1–21) and surrounding material: the sign of Jonah (Matt 16:1–4) and the healing of a blind man in stages (Mark 8:22–26). For 6th Easter, the gospel (Matt 18:1–20 or Luke 9:46–50; 17:1–4) concerns entering the kingdom humbly, as children, free from stumbling blocks and grudges. On Ascension, Jesus questions those in the temple concerning the identity of the Messiah, David's Son (Mark 12:35–37 or Luke 20:41–47). In the event that Ascension Thursday is not observed, these shorter texts may be included on 7th Easter, when Jesus cuts off the chief priests, scribes, and elders when they question his authority (Mark 12:35–37; Luke 20:41–47).

Finally, one Johannine resurrection text (21:20–25) remains unassigned by the *RCL*, namely, the epilogue to the fourth gospel and the hyperbolic declaration that "if every one of [the things Jesus did] were written down, . . . the world itself could not contain the books that would be written." This text, while not directly linked to any other lection in the season, should also be considered as an optional gospel reading for the 4th–7th Sundays of Easter.

For Pentecost, in a Matthean passage from Jesus' missionary discourse, he urges the disciples to be "innocent as doves," and not to prepare their testimonies in advance, since it is "the Spirit of your Father speaking through you" (Matt 10:9–23). The Lukan option also concerns public testimony—shouting from the rooftops what has been heard behind closed doors—and warns against the one and only unforgiveable sin: blasphemy against the Holy Spirit (Luke 12:1–12).

Trinity Sunday draws on the last of the unused Johannine material from Jesus' farewell discourse (15:18—16:4a). Of these verses, only 15:26–27 have been used in the *RCL*, but they are retained here so as to maintain a Trinitarian and testimonial focus and to avoid disrupting the canonical form of the text (despite their digressive quality). Daunting as is this text (esp. 16:1–4a), which speaks of the world's hatred of Jesus and his disciples, it is simply foolish and dangerous in our present situation to ignore it, especially in light of the challenges faced by the persecuted church today.

With the season of Resurrection, the epistle sequence commences semicontinuously through the vast and often challenging material omitted from 2 Corinthians. With the exception of Ascension Thursday, this series spans all the Sundays of Easter, as well as Pentecost, and finally concludes on Trinity Sunday, when the popular Trinitarian benediction (2 Cor 13:13) serves as a fitting conclusion.

Resurrection Sunday is an opportune occasion to preach the great litany of "consolation" with which Paul opens this letter. Although resurrection is not the explicit focus of the passage, the implications of the resurrection ring loud and clear for those who, like Paul, have "despaired of life itself," and now "rely . . . on God who raises the dead" (1:8–9). For Resurrection Evening, missing verses are gathered from chapters that only receive a partial treatment in the *RCL*; these verses address "the ministry of the Spirit," and the Spirit as our "guarantee," as "we groan, longing to be clothed with our heavenly dwelling." On 2nd Easter, Paul's conciliatory tone, in recalling his previous disciplinary visit and the pain it caused both him and the church, gives way to a glorious celebration of the fragrant presence of knowing Christ "from life to life" in the midst of the Christian journey, and ends with the assertion that "we speak as persons of sincerity, . . . sent from God and standing in his presence" (1:23—2:17). The selection for 3rd Easter (6:11—7:1) is by far the most difficult and problematic from a rhetorical and source-critical perspective. Yet, with proper research and contextualization (i.e., in light of 1 Cor 5:9; et al.), this passage is an important reminder that the foregoing eschatological statements regarding a new creation are not to be universally applied without regard to the ongoing need for personal holiness and the fear of God. The epistle for 4th Easter (7:2–16) frames its discussion of the benefits of godly grief in terms of joy and consolation and the fruits of earnestness and sincerity, while the lections for 5th and 6th Easter afford an opportunity to preach on stewardship (8:1—9:15) in the season of Resurrection, as opposed to an autumnal "harvest" season. The nature of true apostolic authority and the "weapons" of spiritual militancy (10:1–18), the singular character of the gospel, the danger of false prophets and satanic deception, the missional reality of suffering (11:1–33), the aim of building up the church (12:11–21), and the need for self-examination (13:1–10) punctuate the provocative final chapters of 2 Corinthians which are assigned for 7th Easter, Pentecost, and Trinity Sunday.

Where the psalms for Easter morning and evening are concerned, Psalm 71 is added to Psalms 75 and 76 as an option that appears to speak of the hope of resurrection as clearly as any psalm, or any other Old Testament text, for that matter (see esp. 71:20).

There are few, if any, explicit connections worth mentioning between the psalms selected for the season; indeed, many of the chosen psalms (e.g., Psalms 64, 60, 108, 129) appear to have no direct bearing on the New Testament. Yet, amidst their militaristic images and pleas for defense and protection from dread enemies, including death itself, certain words of assurance arise that resound with the hope of eternal life: "God will ransom my soul from the power of Sheol, for he will receive me" (Ps 49:15). On three occasions (2nd Easter, Ascension, and Pentecost), unused sections from the great acrostic Torah psalm (119:73–96, 113–136, 145–176) are proposed. Here the intent is not to force or overload particular allusions (e.g., cf. Ps 119:120 and Luke 12:5), but simply to allow this marvelous psalm, which otherwise repels rather than attracts (by virtue of its size and gravity), to function anew as an endless source of illumination, perhaps for prayers before the reading and preaching of the Word.

With a continuous reading of the epistle under way and the gospels didactically occupied with resurrection themes, the Old Testament lections in this season play more of an *ad hoc*, supporting role, as is the case in much of Year D.[12] Several selections from Deuteronomy are suggested:

| Easter Day | Deut 7:1–26 (cf. 7:9; 2 Cor 1:18) |
| | *Theological purity to be enforced in the conquest of Canaan* |

---

12. This is not to suggest such a role is normative for the Old Testament. On the contrary, a fully canonical lectionary will inevitably provide for seasons in which the Old Testament, in continuous or semicontinuous fashion, is the primary focus and suggests the selection of other texts.

Easter Evening	Deut 9:8–21 (cf. 9:10; 2 Cor 3:3, 7) *God's anger and mercy in the incident of the golden calf*
6th Easter	Deut 15:1–18 (cf. 15:10; 2 Cor 9:7) *The sabbatical year for cancelling debts and releasing slaves* OR Deut 19:15–21 (cf. 19:15; Matt 18:16) *The* lex talionis *in light of bearing false witness*
Pentecost	Deut 5:1–15 (6–21) 22–33 *The giving of the Ten Commandments at Pentecost* OR Deut 31:23–29 *The placement of the law as witness, warning against apostasy*

Other Torah passages that inform the epistle and gospel readings:

Easter Evening	Exod 34:29–34 (cf. 34:30, 33–35; 2 Cor 3:7, 10, 13, 16) *The radiant face of Moses*
4th Easter	Gen 38:1–30 (cf. 38:8; Matt 22:24; Mark 12:19) *Tamar and Judah (the "kinsman redeemer")*
Pentecost	Exod 4:1–17 (cf. 4:12; Matt 10:19) *Signs for Moses and the promise of inspired testimony*

Several passages from both the former prophets and the latter prophets play a typological or promise/fulfillment role. First, from the Samuel and Kings literature:

5th Easter	1 Sam 21:1–15 *David on the run (the showbread at Nob; asylum in Gath)* OR 2 Kgs 4:38–44 *Elisha purifies a poisoned stew, feeds one hundred with twenty loaves*
Trinity	1 Kgs 9:1–9; 11:1–13 *The* LORD's *reply to Solomon's prayer of dedication; Solomon's folly as an "interfaith" syncretist*

Excerpts from the latter prophets include the following:

2nd Easter	Hos 14:1–9 *The* LORD *will restore and renew a repentant Israel*
3rd Easter	Zech 13:1–9 (cf. 13:7; John 16:32) *Promise of a cleansing fountain; prophesy of the stricken shepherd*
7th Easter	Jer 9:23–24; 24:1–10 (cf. 2 Cor 10:8–17) *Boasting in the* LORD; *the good and bad figs*
Pentecost	Dan 12:1–13 (cf. 12:12; Matt 10:22) *Endurance to the end*

Finally, selections from the Wisdom literature are also represented:

4th Easter	Eccl 5:1–20 *"God is in heaven, and you upon earth . . ."*
Ascension	Prov 1:1–7 *Wisdom, knowledge, and instruction: "The fear of the LORD"*
Trinity	Eccl 8:1–17 *Even the wise do not know what God is doing, but "it will be well with those who fear God"*

THE SUNDAYS AFTER TRINITY/ORDINARY TIME

ORDINARY TIME (9TH–14TH ORDINARY)

Ordinary Time in Year D is anything but ordinary, as it allocates nearly the entire remainder of the year to a sequential reading through the last days of Jesus' ministry: the apocalyptic discourse (15th–19th Ordinary) the confrontations between Jesus and the religious authorities in Jerusalem prior to his arrest and suffering (20th–23rd), and the passion narratives themselves (24th–33rd). While the gospels drive many selections for Ordinary Time, the epistles often do so as well, as the two courses take a complementary yet largely independent parallel track. Meanwhile, six weeks lie between Trinity and the commencement of the gospel series.

With the exception of one Johannine option (John 5:31–47) suggested for 13th Ordinary (and Epiphany), where Jesus speaks of the witnesses who testify to him, the gospel lections for these weeks are drawn from the Synoptics; taken together they suggest (perhaps more in hindsight than by intention or design) a chiastic structure:

9th Ordinary: Matt 17:9–20 OR Mark 9:9–29 OR Luke 9:18–27 (28–36) 37–45
Fragments related to the transfiguration: the "messianic secret," exorcism of a mute boy

   10th Ordinary: Matt 12:22–37 OR Luke 1:14–23
   Exorcisms, a house divided, binding the strong man, good vs. bad tree/fruit; judgment for every careless word

      11th Ordinary: Matt 13:10–17 (18–33) 34–35 OR Mark 4:1–25 OR Luke 8:4–25; 13:18–21
      Jesus' "explanation" (Isaianic rationale) for his use of parables; the hiddenness of the seed/word; the light of the world

      12th Ordinary: Matt 15:1–20 OR Mark 7:1–20
      Human tradition vs. the Word of God; out of the heart, the mouth speaks

13th Ordinary: Matt 9:27–34 OR John 5:31–47
Exorcisms, healing of blind men; the witnesses to Jesus

14th Ordinary: Matt 12:38–50 OR Luke 11:24–36
"Something greater . . . is here!"; healthy eyes admit light, but an evil generation asks for a sign; the unclean spirit that returns with others.

The epistle readings here are a selection of unused portions of letters that the *RCL* has otherwise explored fairly thoroughly. A quick comparison with the gospel themes listed above reveals commonalities worth investigating.

9th Ordinary	Phil 2:14–30	*Imitation of Christ as innocent, blameless children of God, who "shine like stars in the world"*
10th Ordinary	1 John 3:8–15; 4:1–6	*". . . test the spirits to see whether they are of God!"*
11th Ordinary	Eph 4:17–25; 5:3–7	*The need to repudiate pagan ways, to "be renewed in the spirit of your minds," and to put on "the new self," or risk hardness of heart. Some things should never be mentioned, but thanksgiving is always appropriate.*
11th Ordinary	2 Pet 2:1–22	*False teachers and their destruction*
12th Ordinary	1 Tim 4:1–16	*Apostasy and demonic teaching in the last days contrasted with the good minister of Christ, who is devoted to public reading of Scripture, exhorting, and teaching*
13th Ordinary	1 Cor 3:12–15; 4:6–21	*The builder's work will be tested by fire; "already you have all you want!" The apostolic life is a spectacle, the apostle a fool for Christ's sake; "nothing beyond what is written."*
13th Ordinary	2 John 1–13	*Walking in the truth; love defined as walking in the commandments; warning against "going beyond" the teaching of Christ*
14th Ordinary	1 Cor 5:1—6:11	*". . . your body is a temple of the Holy Spirit within you."*

The psalms for the beginning of Ordinary Time are Psalms 142, 74, 7, 55, 56, and either 57 or 3; all but one (Psalm 74) are individual laments. Apart from a solitary conditional warning about the consequences of failing to repent (cf. Ps 7:14; Luke 13:3), no explicit allusions or quotations drive these selections. Rather, one may simply listen to the plaintive, lonely cry of the psalmist (Psalm 142) juxtaposed with the deliverance of a mute boy from an unclean spirit and his restoration to a desperate father. Might such a prayer (the Davidic superscription notwithstanding) be the prayer of many voiceless youths in the grip of overpowering forces? Might not these several censored protests against the worldly violence and scheming enemies (Psalms 3, 55–57, and 74) finally be permitted to resound in the presence of gospel texts that also seek a hearing as they speak of genuinely irreconcilable differences between clean and unclean spirits, good and bad fruit, evil and pure hearts, holiness and profanity, Satan and Jesus Christ? If so, the church may just recover a healthy sense of the ongoing relevance of the sacred/secular divide (Wainwright), the demise of which has been greatly exaggerated, even falsely proclaimed and foolishly lauded, in recent generations.

Two Old Testament options are suggested for the 9th and 10th Sundays of Ordinary Time, each involving consecutive texts from either the Song of Moses (Deut 31:30—32:43) with its epilogue (32:44–47), or the six "woes" (Isaiah 5:8–24) that follow the Song of the Vineyard (5:1–7). Both songs (or song fragments) are divided in two, for one can scarcely absorb either in a single application. Yet each is vitally important for interpreting troubling times and for restoring categorical clarity when all such criteria appear lost on "a perverse and crooked generation" (cf. Deut 32:5; Matt 17:17; Phil 2:15).

Several options for 11th Ordinary lend perspective to Jesus' obscure explanation regarding his use of parables: the substance of the message given to Isaiah (6:8–13) at his commissioning (to which all four evangelists refer); the messianic allegory of the cedar (Ezek 17:22–24); and, by contrast, the humiliation of Pharoah (Ezek 31:1–18) and Nebuchadnezzar (Dan 4).

For 12th Ordinary is proposed either Isaiah 29 or Isaiah 59, both of which resonate far beyond the spatial and temporal borders of ancient Israel, promising restoration to a repentant nation, but not without vividly contrasting the vile, corrupt stupidity of her leaders (cf. Isa 29:13; Matt 15:8–9; Mark 7:6–7) with the LORD's militant intervention for the sake of his name and for the sake of his children.

Three texts have been paired, somewhat mechanically, with the epistle lections for 13th Ordinary. The apostle's joy at those "walking in the truth" (2 John 4) recalls Hezekiah's poignant plea for healing (2 Kgs 20:3), while the fiery testing of the builder's work (1 Cor 3:13–15) reflects the LORD's willing ability to snatch the repentant from the fire—if only they *would* repent! (Amos 4:11; cf. Mal 4:1)

For 14th Ordinary, coupled with Jesus' observation that a healthy eye illumines the whole body (Matt 12:29; Luke 11:33–36) and with his awakening words "something greater . . . is here" (Matt 12:41–42; cf. 12:6; Luke 11:31–32), is the eye-opening revelation to Elisha's servant that many horses and fiery chariots outnumber the "great" Aramean army (2 Kgs 6).

THE APOCALYPTIC DISCOURSE (15TH–19TH ORDINARY)

The Apocalyptic or Olivet discourse only coheres as such (i.e., as a single discourse) in Matthew (24–25) and Mark (13), with Luke distributing parallel sayings over several chapters. For the first three of these five weeks, either Matthew or Mark may be read in continuous fashion, although for a more complete reading, a slight detour is required on 16th Ordinary to gather up a handful of Matthean verses (10:17–22b) that appear in the missionary discourse. (The interchangeability of this missionary instruction with warnings of extreme persecution should not be overlooked.) In a certain sense, these three weeks may all be gathered under the eschatological heading "not yet" (Matt 24:6), since the temple's destruction and the beginnings of birthpangs are but signs that come *before* the end, as do the persecutions, the desolating sacrilege, and the appearance of many false messiahs and false prophets.

Matthew's Gospel takes the lead with 18th Ordinary, since it includes the Markan material, but adds certain details regarding the "coming of the Son of Man" (24:27, 30), namely, "the sign of the Son of Man" in heaven, the mourning of "all the tribes of the earth" (v. 30), and the "loud trumpet call" (v. 31). The selection also includes the parable of the fig tree, as well as promises that the present generation will see these things fulfilled and that, though heaven and earth will pass away, Jesus' words will not (vv. 32–35). The Lukan parallel differs in at least two important ways: it is a response to a question posed not by the disciples, but by the Pharisees, and it includes a unique "already" saying that, by itself, redirects all futuristic concern into the present existential moment: "The kingdom of God is not coming with things that can be observed; nor will they say, 'Look,

here it is!' or 'There it is!' For, in fact, the kingdom of God is among you"
(17:20–21). Tempting as it is to let that be the final word on all matters
apocalyptic (*à la* "realized eschatology"), that does not begin to address
all that Jesus says to his disciples afterwards (v. 22–37). It is also, perhaps
too readily and unadvisedly, to take one's seat with the Pharisees.

A complete reading would include, on 19th Ordinary, the pericope
with which the three-year cycle begins, Matthew 24:36–44 (Advent 1,
Year A), but the primary aim here is to afford the conclusion of the chapter a fair hearing, where Jesus identifies "the faithful and wise slave" as
the one who gives the others "their allowance of food at the proper time"
(*en kairoi*). Clearly, Jesus did not have lectionary terminology (i.e., "propers") in mind here, but the suggestion is not as absurd as it sounds, since
synagogue worship has always involved reading Scripture systematically.
Neither are we justified in boiling his meaning down to temporal food
only, not when he himself understands food (*broma* [John 4:34; cf. Matt
14:15]) as doing the will of God, the word of God itself as more vital than
bread (*artoi* [Matt 4:4]), and life more important than food (*trophe* [6:25;
cf. 24:45]). On the contrary, here is the precise prescription for those who
find these apocalyptic texts unsettling. Jesus tells us what to do in the interim between the Pharisaical "already" and the dispensational "not yet,"
saying, in a sense, "When I come, let me find you, wisely and faithfully,
giving the others their (scriptural, missional) food at the proper time."
Preachers, take note!

The epistle readings have already turned to a semicontinuous
course of omitted sections of 1 Corinthians, beginning with 13th
Ordinary. On 15th Ordinary, Paul's lengthy chapter on sexual relations
makes reference to "the impending crisis" (7:26) and suggests a way of
life that suspends the present order of things, that is, to live "as though
. . . not" married, mourning, rejoicing, buying, or dealing with the
world, "for the present form of this world is passing away" (vv. 29–31).
Although modern exegetes often dismiss Paul's imminent eschatology
as mistaken or mistimed, there may well be a profound therapeutic
sense in framing sexual matters, a source of anxiety for many, in the
eschatological light of mortality and eternity.

The course runs through 17th Ordinary, when, as the gospels warn
of the desolating sacrilege, Paul contrasts the worship of demons and idols
with the worship of Christ (10:14–22). On 18th Ordinary, the Corinthian
sequence is interrupted with three options that, again in concert with the

gospels, address the reality of false prophets and false messiahs (or anti-christs): 1 John 2:3–29; 2 John 1–13; or 2 Peter 2:1–22.

With 19th Ordinary, the epistle returns to 1 Corinthians 11. Although the topic of proper dress and headcoverings in public worship (vv. 1–16) is daunting to say the least, our generation, more than most, may be in need of some biblical teaching on the subject. More importantly, if faithfully feeding the household of God demonstrates wisdom (Matt 24:45), then surely the least that the servants of the Lord who are fed at his table can do is to practice self-examination and discernment of the body, and to strive for unity and integrity in the church (vv. 17–34). Indeed, the neglect of this communion text, once such a prominent—and properly penitential—part of the sacramental liturgy in the Reformed tradition, has undoubtedly contributed to the fractious state of the church and its denominations today. To use the words of institution (vv. 23–26) as we do, divorced from the rebuke (vv. 17–25) and the warnings (vv. 27–32) in which they are nested, would be laughable if it were not so tragic. Perhaps placing them in an apocalyptic context is precisely what is needed at this juncture.

If, as is often noted, the Bible's apocalyptic literature emerged under persecution, the lament psalms, with their complaints against relentless enemies, express a similar plea for justice and hope for deliverance. Several lament psalms are suggested for this series. For 15th Ordinary, an unused fragment from an individual lament implores the LORD to react swiftly when protecting the psalmist against those who hunt him mercilessly: "Guard me as the apple of the eye" (Ps 17:8). Surprisingly, when taken in earnest, the psalmist actually asks provision for his enemies and their children "whose portion in life is in this world" (v. 14). That qualification, of course, presumes the enemies' mortality and lack of any eternal inheritance. Meanwhile, stripped of irony, it is a remarkable example of praying for one's enemies. An alternative selection for this week is a communal lament (Ps 83), which cries for deliverance from an alliance of surrounding nations bent on a familiar and all too contemporary theme: wiping Israel out as a nation (v. 4). Perhaps better assigned to 17th Ordinary (cf. Luke 21:20), this lament seeks divine intervention in international affairs, especially when Israel is the target of conspiracies. The names may have changed, but the spirits have not, for there is "nothing new under the sun" (Eccl 1:9). Nevertheless, here too, nested among many hyperbolic cries for God to overthrow the enemies ("Fill their faces with shame") is this purposeful rationale: "so that they may seek your name, O LORD" (Ps 83:16). Truly, the laments are not unmitigated curses and invectives, but with patient, pastoral, purposeful attention—"greater attention" (Heb 2:1)—they reveal their intercessory nature.

Psalm 54, suggested for 16th Ordinary, is another individual lament that, if anything, is amazingly sparing in its use of imperatives directed against the enemies. Most of its godward imperatives simply plead on the psalmist's own behalf: "save me," "vindicate me," "hear my prayer," "give ear to the words of my mouth" (54:1–2). When it comes to what God will do to the enemies, indicative expressions of faith (v. 5a, 7b) outnumber the solitary (imperative) call for their destruction, which itself is framed and qualified in terms of God's covenant faithfulness: "In your faithfulness, put an end to them" (v. 5b). Such a psalm well complements the gospel warnings of persecutions.

Unused fragments of either of two psalms are suggested for 17th Ordinary, when the gospel reading foretells the desolating sacrilege and the flight from Judea, and (more hopefully) promises that the days of unprecedented suffering have *already* been cut short (Mark 13:14–20). The two psalms suggested for this week, however, are not laments, but are (in some respects) covenantal. In the omitted verses of Psalm 50 (vv. 16–21), God rebukes the wicked for hating discipline, speaking evil, slandering kin, and presuming too much familiarity with God. Clearly, the proper response to such a rebuke is repentance, even for people of faith. Bernard Anderson classifies this psalm as a "covenant renewal liturgy," which is fitting in light of its more favorable verses that declare *thanksgiving* to be the sacrifice God desires (vv. 14, 23; cf. v. 5). Thus, if Psalm 50 is chosen, there is no reason why the entire psalm should not be used. In this same vein, Psalm 105 is a thanksgiving, storytelling psalm that celebrates God's covenantal faithfulness to the patriarchs in preserving them from famine and rescuing them from Egyptian bondage. Although most of the psalm is used in Year A, the sections relating to amorous kings (vv. 12–15; cf. Gen 12:10–20; 20:1–17; 26:1–11)[13] and the plagues of Egypt have been omitted (vv. 27–36). Such full, even fulsome, recitations of the *mirabilia*

---

13. "Genesis thought that a patriarch passing his wife off as his sister was so important that it tells such a story three times, and a recent feminist interpretation offers an intriguing suggestion as to the reason." Goldingay, "Canon and Lection," 96–97; Goldingay's reference is to Exum, *Fragmented Women*, 148–69.

Dei are typical of covenant renewal rites, however, and are not enhanced by attenuating the contrast.

On 18th Ordinary, another individual lament (Ps 59) promises songs in praise of God's strength and steadfast love in return for deliverance from the howling, prowling enemies plotting with bloodthirst against the psalmist. Again, as worship glorifies God and as God's glory is best revealed in contrast, here is a doxology for the coming of the Son of Man into a world teeming with antichrists: the psalmist's vow to sing (vv. 16–17) is a song itself, one that ascends far above the beastly and guttural curses of ravenous enemies (vv. 1–5).

The psalm for 19th Ordinary is again an unused fragment, albeit a large one, from Psalm 37, an alphabetic acrostic in the wisdom tradition. In some respects, it is more a series of proverbs, with the omitted verses (vv. 12–38) contrasting the righteous and the wicked. Yet these verses advance no abstract moral philosophy, but are punctuated with strong theological assurances: "the LORD upholds the righteous," "the LORD knows the days of the blameless," "the LORD holds us by the hand," "the LORD loves justice" and "will exalt you to inherit the land" (vv. 17, 18, 24, 28, 34). Similarly, the gospel portrayal of the faithful and wise servant feeding the other slaves is well suited to the nourishing imagery we find in vv. 19, 25–26.

Selections from Genesis, Deuteronomy, and the latter prophets serve as the Old Testament lections in this series of five weeks. On 15th Ordinary, Jeremiah's temple sermon predicts the destruction of the first temple (7:14), just as Jesus' Olivet discourse predicts the destruction of the second (Matt 24:2; Mark 13:2). Another possibility is Daniel's discernment and interpretation of Nebuchadnezzar's vision of the imperial statue (Dan 2:1–49), which (in LXX) twice includes the strong prophetic phrase *dei genesthai*, "it will happen" (2:28, 45; cf. Matt 24:6; Mark 13:7; Luke 21:9; Rev 1:1, 19; 22:6). Though but an idiomatic link, its use in prophetic texts that declare an end to corrupt objects, places, and practices of worship should not be missed.

On 16th Ordinary, texts are suggested that show direct connections with the missionary section of the gospel narrative (Matt 10:17–22a). The preface to the Song of Moses (Deut 31:23–29) clearly explains its corrective, prophetic, haunting function: it is for a "time to come [when] trouble will befall you" (v. 29).[14] The Torah itself will serve as a witness against rebellious Israel (v. 26), while the missionaries of Christ will testify before kings and Gentiles (Matt 10:18; cf. 2 Cor 3:2–3). Micah's prophecy of family division (7:6) is quoted in Matthew's missionary passage (10:21) and is suggested here to provide depth and context for understanding not only a futuristic prophecy, but the sort of domestic chaos that many people of faith experience every day. The closing section of Daniel (11:40—12:13) is proposed here for the abundance of figures, allusions, and commonalities (exploited by some, unexamined by others) that stand between these apocalyptic writings old and new; above all, especially in the face of all that we do not understand concerning these texts, the call for endurance to the end bears repeating (Dan 12:12; Mark 13:13; 1 Cor 9:12).

Four options are suggested for 17th Ordinary to juxtapose with the prophecy of the desolating sacrilege and the flight from Judea: first, the creedal assertion of the uniqueness of the Lord, his victory over all the gods of the nations, and his love for Israel's ancestors (Deut 4:32–40); second, an oracle of the separation of the servants of God from the wicked who have forsaken him (Isa 65:10–16; cf. v. 11; 1 Cor 10:21); third, an oracle of approaching judgment (Ezek 7:1–27; cf. v. 16 and Matt 24:16; though several possibilities from Ezek 8–10 are also worth considering); and fourth, Zechariah's vision of the Lord standing on the Mount of Olives (Zech 14:4–9).

The destruction of Sodom and Gomorrah (Gen 19) is suggested for 18th Ordinary in light of the dramatic theme of divine rescue from oppression by the lawless and the allusions found in 2 Peter 2:6–7 to this once overused, now censored text. But let the preacher beware: there is nothing in the epistle to suggest that certain kinds of lawlessness and licentiousness are any better or worse than others; none is exempted, none considered "blessings." When reading this text in conversation with the apocalyptic discourse, let the primary emphasis fall, not on the fearful prospect of judgment, but on the preventive admonition "do not look back" (v. 17), and on the Lord's provision for the one to whom he shows

---

14. Whatever one thinks of Day's handling of the imprecatory psalms, which I think must be taken in light of its own highly exceptional presuppositions, it is certainly symptomatic of the current state of affairs that a conservative thinker such as Day may claim that the Song of Moses is "central to the theology and hope of all Scripture," while not a single verse of it, or a single reference to it, appears in the *RCL*. See Day, *Crying for Justice*, 59.

mercy, to whom the angel says, "I can do nothing until you arrive there," that is, take shelter in Zoar (v. 21).

Finally, for 19th Ordinary, Genesis 6:1–8 is suggested, for want of other texts to aid in understanding the peculiarities of the epistle (1 Cor 11:10). A better possibility is Zechariah 9:1–8 (11–12) 13–17. This envelope surrounding the famous Palm Sunday oracle (vv. 9–10) speaks of the LORD's overthrowing Israel's enemies (Tyre, Ashkelon, Gaza, Ekron, Philistia, Greece), and his glorious ingathering of his scattered people for the sake of "the blood of [his] covenant" (v. 11).

PRELUDE TO THE PASSION (20TH–23RD ORDINARY)

In narrative terms, the apocalyptic discourse, dramatic as it is, actually suspends the action of the gospel, as discourses tend to do. It is a lengthy didactic insertion, couched in question/answer mode, at some remove from the drama in Jerusalem proper. In the Synoptics, Passion Week follows this sequence:

1. triumphal entry (to Jerusalem)

2. conflict with authorities (in the vicinity of the temple complex)

3. apocalyptic discourse (Mount of Olives, east of the temple)

4. the passion narrative (starts in Bethany, ends in Jerusalem)

In the case of Year D, the second and third stages of the narrative are reversed so as to establish greater continuity with the Passion itself. In a four-week prelude to the Passion, various unused gospel texts have been assigned that depict the growing tension with the authorities. While the Matthean and Markan conflicts belong to the sequence outlined above, two selections from John and one from Luke do not. Nevertheless, they find a place in Year D, as they are either muted or absent from the *RCL*, and are placed here in keeping with the general trajectory of the conflict that leads to the arrest, trial, and crucifixion of Jesus.

First, Jesus' barrage of seven woes to the scribes, Pharisees, hypocrites, and blind guides (Matt 23:13–36) is slated for 20th Ordinary. In Luke (11:37–54), half of his six "woes" are reserved for "you lawyers [who] have taken away the key of knowledge; you did not enter yourselves, and you hindered those who were entering" (v. 52). This is strong stuff; one can understand why preachers and lectionary committees shrink from it. But the preacher's crisis is something that must be worked out with fear and trembling (Phil 2:12) *outside* the pulpit, without making the sermon about oneself, without luring the listener into pacifying the pious preacher so deeply moved by his or her own sin; that is precisely the stumbling block to be avoided here: oneself. Better by far to keep the focus on the conduct that earns Jesus' wrath here and fill the yawning gap left by the *RCL* that leaves us wondering what Jesus' intense lament, "Jerusalem, Jerusalem" (Matt 23:37), is all about, for the opening verses of the chapter (23:1–12) can scarcely account for the vehemence of his anguish at the end.

On 21st Ordinary, the twofold incident of Jesus' cleansing the temple and cursing a fig tree has been selected (Matt 21:12–22; Mark 11:12–25). Oddly, the *RCL* includes no synoptic accounts of Jesus' driving out the moneychangers, favoring the Johannine version instead (Lent 3, Year B); but two evangelists assume a close connection between the temple cleansing and the withering of the fig tree, the latter bearing no mention in the *RCL* except in Luke's parabolic form (6:1–9; Lent 3, Year C). Evidently, the lectionary committee felt the need to put the poor fig tree at some distance from Jesus, both in parabolic space and by a span of one year in time! But why do Matthew and Mark tie these events together? Certain interpreters probably overload the allegorical connection to Israel (Hos 9:10), but if anyone is led to exploit it, the olive tree analogy of Romans (11:13–32) should restrain those who are tempted to boast. More than an indictment of Israel, the cursing of the fig tree has to do with fruitless leaders who scatter God's people, scuttle the prayer that is the essence of worship, profiteer from the cultic system, and produce only fig leaves, the aboriginal means of hiding from God. The temple cult has departed so far from the LORD's purpose that when Jesus sees a tree that (like the temple) is all "coverage" and no fruit, he blasts it. The fig leaves don't stand a chance.

The next two Sundays (22nd and 23rd Ordinary) take up unused portions of John (10:10–21, 31–42, and 11:46–57). The first concerns the response of the Jews to Jesus at the winter Festival of the Dedication (but this detail is not mentioned in the omitted verses and need not distract from the plot). Jesus is threatened with stoning, accused of equating himself with God; his reply asserts his Sonship in relation to the Father, but this, he says, is nothing compared to what the Scriptures say, which (he declares) "cannot be annulled": "you are gods!" (John 10:35; Ps 82:6). This is exegetically and theological thorny, to be sure. Jesus does not divinize humans here, but refers to "those to whom the word of God came" (10:35). The setting of the psalm in question is crucial (82:1). More to the point here is that his claims regarding himself can be trusted, as can the good works that he does in the Father's name. It is a story of some rejecting him (vv. 19–20, 31, 33, 39) and others coming to faith (vv. 21, 41–42); it is also a passage that clearly asserts the divinity of the Son prior to his suffering.

The final gospel text in the prelude to the Passion contains the prophecy of the corrupt high priest Ciaphas, which the evangelist asserts was nonetheless true (11:49–52). The setting here is important: the raising of Lazarus has inspired a fear that fuels the conspiracy against Jesus (11:46–48). The closing section sets the stage for the Passion: "Now the Passover of the Jews was near" (v 55). The interpretation of the evangelist offers a memorable distillation of the gospel: "Jesus was about to die for the nation, and not for the nation only, but to gather into one the dispersed children of God" (vv. 51–52).

Where the epistle is concerned, the continuous reading of 1 Corinthians is interrupted for two more weeks. With three excluded chapters of 1 Timothy to work with, 20th Ordinary (when in the gospels Jesus directs his breathtaking "woes" at the corrupt authorities) seems an opportune time to include 1 Tim 3:1–16, with its list of the spiritual qualifications for church leadership, that is, the offices of bishop and deacon, and for the lovely Christ hymn with which the chapter concludes.

On 21st Ordinary, as Jesus commends the power of faith to his disciples after cursing the fruitless fig tree (and vacuous worship with it), Colossians 2 speaks of faith as the power through which God raised us with Jesus from a baptismal death (2:11–12); it offers "the riches of assured understanding" and "the treasures of wisdom and knowledge" in Christ (2:2–3), among which is the assurance that the record of our sins and the demands of the law are erased (vv. 13–14). The joyful gospel of forgiveness is here, along with freedom from empty, mechanical, legalistic religion (vv. 20–23), all of which may come through more clearly by omitting the verses that have been parenthetically included in the RCL (2:16–19).

With the final two weeks of the prelude to the Passion, the semicontinuous reading of 1 Corinthians concludes as well. Lengthy as it is, this is the one opportunity for 1 Corinthians 14—despite its text-critical problems, yet so basic to our understanding of worship!—to gain a hearing, for it is otherwise entirely excluded from the RCL. One will likely need to choose carefully which verses to include, since the gift of tongues and the role of women are not at present burning issues in many mainline churches; yet upbuilding and order, clarity and coming to faith are at stake here, and though there are no explicit connections between this chapter and the selected gospel or psalms, it is quite possible that these texts will strike similar notes, along similar lines.

First Corinthians 16 is suggested for 23rd Ordinary. With no direct references to the gospel or the psalm, it is simply a matter of how committed one is to the course of the epistle and how thoroughly one needs to conclude it. The closing salutations are not usually the most exciting passages, yet they often lend a sense of concreteness (owing to specific names and circumstances mentioned), and inspire a sense of succession or commissioning. The chapter is rich in missional sensibilities (vv. 1–12) and doxological blessings (vv. 13, 20, 23–24); it even contains a hair-raising curse at the end (v. 22)—not what one expects to find at the end of a letter that includes the famous "love chapter" (13), but effective in making its positive point nonetheless: this is a letter between lovers of Jesus; to all others, hands off and beware!

The psalms for this conflicted prelude consist of individual laments, a portion of a "Zion liturgy" or communal thanksgiving, and a communal lament that is one of the most violent psalms of imprecation (Ps 58). The latter is paired with texts for 20th Ordinary, specifically with the contrast between proper conduct in "the church of the living God" (1 Tim 3:15) and the hypocritical corruption denounced by Jesus' "woes" (Matt 23:13–39). Great care and caution are always needed when handling the more vitriolic psalms, but (as with Ps 82) the proper framework is established in terms of the first verse, not in terms of demythologizing presuppositions. To take it literally is to take it spiritually; those addressed, denounced, and cursed are the capricious, unjust "gods"—*enemy* gods—who "deal out violence on earth" (Ps 58:1–2), the elemental spirits from whose influence those baptized into Christ are now freed (see Col 2:20; 21st Ordinary).

Psalms 140, 120, and 141 (21st–23rd Ordinary, respectively) are each individual laments that implore the LORD for deliverance from personal enemies. Psalm 120 is the prayer of an exile, who lives among the violent and seeks deliverance "from lying lips (and) a deceitful tongue"(v. 2). His is a song of woe at being surrounded by "those who hate peace" (v. 6), but since the psalms are rarely univocal, we have no assurance that it is the psalmist and not the LORD himself who speaks the sentence against the deceitful tongue (vv. 3–4).

Psalm 140 makes even more frequent reference to the continual "hot" warfare of the wicked. Again, however, the prayer of the psalmist is remarkably restrained. Primarily defensive (vv. 1, 4), it petitions the LORD to frustrate the plans of the wicked (v. 8), asking for justice in kind: let what the wicked have planned to do to the psalmist backfire on them. Granted, this is more an expression of *lex talionis* (the retaliatory code that calls for "an eye for an eye") than of turning the other cheek, but the lack of escalation is nevertheless arresting.[15]

In Psalm 141, the violence of the enemy is less a frontal assault than a covert plot to ensnare the psalmist, who expresses preference for corporal correction by the righteous to falling into the trap of the wicked. The prayer is a model of spiritual militancy: first and foremost, the psalmist asks for the sanctification of the prayer itself (vv. 1–2), that the works and the thoughts, the mouth, lips, and heart of the psalmist might not go astray (vv. 3–4); second, he expresses willingness to be disciplined, if that will keep him faithful and fixed on God (v. 5a); third, he asks to be kept entirely free from "the oil of the wicked" (v. 5b), a reference, no doubt, to evil spirits that drive the actions of his enemies, and he asserts his opposition to such evil: "for my prayer is continually against their wicked deeds" (v. 5c). Finally, he leaves it to others to condemn them (v. 6a), but professes his faith that, when they are condemned, his own pleasant words will be remembered as such, his righteous and peaceful conduct will be vindicated (v. 6b). It is a prayer appropriate to 23rd Ordinary, when the chief priests and Pharisees fix their resolve "to put [Jesus] to death" (John 11:53). More than that, it is a paradigm of spiritually militant prayer for the wise and mature liturgical assembly whose worship is honestly attuned to the cosmic realities by which it is surrounded and acutely mindful of what is at stake.

An optional fragment for 22nd Ordinary is Psalm 68, which does not fit neatly into any of the more familiar genres, but is undoubtedly and unambiguously militant, an exuberant celebration of God's mighty victories on behalf of his people. The omitted verses (vv. 11–31) definitely lose something when separated from the more popular and less problematic introduction (vv. 1–10) and doxology (vv. 32–35), but the fragment

---

15. For a sobering consideration of the imprecatory psalms and the role of *lex talionis* in an age of terrorism, see Day, *Crying for Justice*, esp. 14–15, 34–35, 66–72, 109–16.

remains coherent nonetheless, even if it is rather gory. Perhaps this psalm above all others demonstrates the principle that the greater glory—"Our GOD is a GOD of salvation, and to GOD, the Lord, belongs escape from death" (v. 20)—is best served by forthrightness, not demureness, when it comes to the end that awaits the archenemies of God: "But GOD will shatter the heads of the enemies, the hairy crown of those who walk in their guilty ways" (v. 21).

The Old Testament selections again include multiple options. For 20th Ordinary, Jeremiah's oracle against the royal house of Judah summons the leaders to justice and righteousness (22:3; cf. Matt 23:23), and though it threatens to make "this house . . . a desolation" (v. 5) if the rulers abandon the covenant and worship other gods (v. 9), it offers hope of continuous reign if the word of the LORD is obeyed (v. 4). The other option for this Sunday, Zechariah 7:1–14, offers similar instruction: "Render true judgments, show kindness and mercy to one another; do not oppress the widow, the orphan, the alien, the poor; and do not devise evil in your hearts against one another" (vv. 9–10). Thus the LORD replies to leaders who come with liturgical questions about fasting (7:1–7), but "they refused to listen . . . and made their hearts adamant in order *not* to hear the law and the words that the LORD of hosts had sent by his spirit through the former prophets. Therefore, great wrath came from the LORD of hosts" (vv. 11–12). Would that Year D included more from the former prophets!

On 21st Ordinary, omitted verses from Genesis 3—the narrative of the original sin—are suggested, in order to recall the figure of the fig tree. The *RCL* is surprisingly narrow in its choice of verses, robbing the story of a great deal of context, but the excluded verses alone make for a rather choppy reading; the entire chapter is best held together. Alternatively, Jeremiah 8:4–13 includes the LORD's lament at Judah's "perpetual backsliding" (v. 5), especially at the careless way in which the prophets and priests have treated the wounded people, "saying, 'Peace, peace,' when there is no peace" (v. 11). The passage concludes with the LORD's complaint: "there are . . . no figs on the fig tree; even the leaves have withered, and what I gave them has passed away from them" (v. 13). Another possibility is Jeremiah's vision of the good and the bad figs (24:1–10), the difference being not that the "good figs," the exiles, have a perfect record of obedience, but that they are wholeheartedly repentant (v. 7), while the "bad figs," the leaders, "the officials," and "those who remain in the land," will become "a horror," for they do not trust the LORD in sending Judah into exile. A final and fourth selection is the prayer of Habakkuk (3:1–19), one of the greatest statements of adoration and faith in the Old Testament, calling upon the LORD to "revive" his work (v. 2), and declaring, "though the fig tree does not blossom, and no fruit is on the vines; . . . yet I will rejoice in the LORD; I will exult in the God of my salvation" (vv. 17–18).

Four Old Testament options are suggested for 22nd Ordinary, each with the epistle in view: first, in light of Paul's emphasis on the desirability of prophecy over tongues, Numbers 11:1–30 records Moses expressing a similar sentiment when a spirit of prophecy was poured upon seventy elders, including two who prophesied outside the camp: "Would that all the LORD's people were prophets, and that the LORD would put his spirit on them!" (11:29) Similarly, Isaiah's oracle of the conversion of the nations (45:14–25) expresses a heuristic acclamation found in the epistle—"God is with you alone, and there is no other; there is no god besides him" (cf. v. 14; 1 Cor 14:25)— and includes a rousing first-person summons from the God who alone can save: "Turn to me and be saved, all the ends of the earth!" (v. 22; cf. John 10:37–38). Zechariah's jealous vision of Zion, with children once again playing safely in the streets, likewise describes many peoples who in future will say to the Jew: "Let us go with you, for we have heard that God is with you" (8:23). Jeremiah 4:19–31 is a simply dreadful text: the prophet sees his land being overrun by a northern invasion and laments, in the voice of the LORD, the foolishness of the people "who do not know me"; rather, they are "skilled in doing evil, but do not know how to do good" (v. 22); the description contrasts sharply with Paul's desire that the Corinthians would be "infants" (i.e., inexperienced) in evil (1 Cor 14:20).

The three options for 23rd Ordinary are, first, the description in Exodus of "the breastpiece of judgment" worn by the high priest (28:15–30), which accompanies the prophecy of Caiaphas; second, the counsel of Ahithophel to Absalom to seek "the life of only one man" (David), advice undercut by Hushai the Archite (2 Sam 15:30–37; 16:15—17:23), a narrative type of the conspiracy hatched against Jesus; and third, Hezekiah's renewal of the Passover festival (2 Chr 30:1–27), which refers to the scorn of those who rejected the king's invitation (v. 10b) and the need for consecration before the festival; happily, it also includes the LORD's gracious answer to Hezekiah's intercession that the irregularities of ritual observance might be overlooked for those who "set their hearts to seek God" (vv. 13–20).

THE PASSION OF OUR LORD JESUS CHRIST (24TH–33RD ORDINARY)

The Passion Narrative has been broken into ten scenes, which includes John's Gospel, but not the lengthy farewell discourse (14–17).

Ordinary	Scene	Texts
24th	I. Anointing at Bethany	Matt 26:1–19 OR Mark 14:16 OR Luke 22:13
25th	II. The Footwashing	John 13:1–20
26th	III. New Commandment	John 13:21–38
27th	IV. The Last Supper	Matt 26:20–35 OR Mark 14:17–31 OR Luke 22:14–38
28th	V. Gethsemane	Matt 26:36–56 OR Mark 14:32–52 OR Luke 22:39–53 OR John 18:1–12
29th	VI. The Sanhedrin; Peter's Denial	Matt 26:57—27:2 OR Mark 14:53—15:1 OR Luke 22:54—23:1 OR John 18:13–28
30th	VII. The Death of Judas; Trial by Pilate	Matt 27:3–31a OR Mark 15:2–20a OR Luke 23:2–25 OR John 18:29—19:16
31st	VIII. The Road to the Cross	Luke 23:26–32
32nd	IX. The Death of Jesus	Matt 27:31b–56 OR Mark 15:20b–41 OR Luke 23:33–49 OR John 19:17–30
33rd	X. The Burial of Jesus	Matt 27:57–66 OR Mark 15:42–47 OR Luke 23:50–56 OR John 19:31–42

Several points warrant explanation. First, selections were made with the assumption that, for the sake of simplicity, the preacher may wish to exercise the Bach option, so to speak, that is, to choose one passion *or* another and stick with it. Granted, certain Sundays offer only one gospel, as when entire blocks (as opposed to a verse or two) of unique material occur (e.g., the Johannine footwashing and new commandment pericopes, the Lukan road to the cross, etc.).

Second, a more comprehensive option would favor the more thorough version, or compile one by drawing from all witnesses for the most inclusive reading. With reference to Aland's *Synopsis of the Four Gospels*, the passages for the ten scenes could be drawn together as follows:[16]

16. With one or two exceptions (Scenes IV and VII), this is the method employed

    I.   Matt 26:1–5; Mark 14:3–9; Luke 22:3–13

   II.   John 13:1–20

  III.   John 13:21–38

  IV.   Luke 22:14–18; Matt 26:26; Luke 22:19b; Matt 26:27–29; Mark 14:18–21; Luke 22:23–30; Matt 26:30–35; Luke 22:31–34; Matt 26:30–35; Luke 22:35–38

   V.   Matt 26:36–56

  VI.   Mark 14:53–15:1

 VII.   Matt 27:3–10; Luke 23:2–25

VIII.   Luke 23:26–32

  IX.   Luke 23:33–49

   X.   John 19:31–37; Luke 23:50–52; Mark 15:44–45; John 19:39–42; Luke 23:55–56

Third, beginnings and endings of selections are not necessarily intended to offer the customary resolution one might expect from a preaching text; on the contrary, the end of a passage may include a transitional verse that serves as a cliffhanger, foreboding what comes next; for example, the trial before the Sanhedrin and the account of Peter's denial end with Jesus being led away to Pilate (Matt 27:2).

Fourth, such a series lends itself to integration, not only with the church calendar (by assigning the account of the Last Supper to World Communion on 27th Ordinary), but with the secular calendar as well. Where many congregations begin a new programmatic or academic year on the Sunday following Labor Day (normally 24th Ordinary), this provides an opportunity for congregations to commence the Passion journey with a renewal of the baptismal covenant.[17]

---

when I preached this series in 2005; the reader of Scripture should bear in mind that when using more than one gospel, the readings need to be carefully compiled together into a single source, since any attempt to flip from one gospel to another in a bound pulpit Bible would be awkward and distracting.

17. Again, when implementing this series in 2005, the service for 24th Ordinary involved a rite of renewal of the baptismal covenant in which people were invited forward to the font; on 27th Ordinary, the Lord's Supper was celebrated, with the people coming forward to receive the elements by intinction (if memory serves), not the normal mode of distribution in this congregation; on 33rd Ordinary, after the readings and a sermon on the burial of Jesus, the people were invited forward once again, to pass by way of the

The epistle readings during the Passion consist of selections from the pastoral epistles and household codes (24th–27th Ordinary) and omitted sections of Romans (28th–33rd Ordinary). The household codes were chosen less for concrete literary connections, and more in keeping with the intimate domestic setting of the gospel scenes in Bethany and in the upper room in Jerusalem. Yet certain themes do coincide: concern for the poor (Matt 26:6–13) and the care of widows (1 Tim 5:3–16); being "subject to one another out of reverence for Christ" (Eph 5:21) and the new commandment of Christ: "love one another" (John 13:34); Paul's reminder that "you serve the Lord Christ," his promise of an inheritance, his emphasis on thanksgiving, his prayer for an opportunity to proclaim "the mystery of Christ," (Col 3:24; 4:2–4)—all of these themes and many more may inspire fresh insight on the Last Supper, perhaps especially where Luke's rich eschatological imagery is recalled. The use of Titus 1:1–16 for 25th Ordinary may be the most peculiar selection for this household sequence, but its sublime prologue (vv. 1–3), its emphasis on trustworthy teaching, the preaching of sound doctrine (v. 9), and the qualitative dialectic between the pure and the impure (v. 15), are too priceless to leave on the cutting room floor.

With 28th Ordinary and the scene in Gethsemane, where "the spirit is willing, but the flesh is weak" (Mark 14:38), the epistle course takes up the remaining fragments of Romans beginning with 7:1–14. Despite Paul's (coincidental) consideration of the enslavement of the flesh to sin in this passage, it is perhaps too much to expect stark correspondence between each epistle selection and each scene in the Passion. Rather, it is characteristic of continuous readings that such courses will run parallel and independently, although as the reader will likely recognize, the great delight of exegesis is the continual discovery of intertextual connections that only the divine author of Scripture can reveal. Thus, there is something fitting in reading Paul's anguished consideration of the Jewish rejection of the Messiah (Rom 9) as Jesus is tried by the Sanhedrin (29th Ordinary), and Paul's discussion of the inclusion of the Gentiles (Rom 10) as Christ appears before the Roman procurator Pilate. With a slight reordering of the Romans sequence,

---

open font, to climb the chancel, step behind the communion table, touch the cross (a permanent fixture on the wall in this New England-style church), and offer personal prayers of thanksgiving. The series of both congregational and personal actions remains one of the most powerful liturgical events in my pastoral memory.

Paul's Christological assertion, "the insults of those who insult you have fallen on me'" (Rom 15:3), accompanies Jesus on the road to the cross (31st Ordinary), while the apostle's admonition, "Do not let what you eat cause the ruin of one for whom Christ died" (Rom 14:15), is read in concert with the accounts of Jesus' death (32nd Ordinary). Finally, there is something undeniably poignant, when reading of Jesus' burial (33rd Ordinary), in hearing the names of the saints in the Roman church, in imagining the wonderful interpersonal connections within the body of Christ, in being assured that "the God of peace will shortly crush Satan under your feet" (Rom 16:20), and in receiving such a doxological benediction as closes the letter—a doxology so exuberant that it fairly throws off the graveclothes of grammar itself (vv. 25–27).

For the anointing at Bethany, Psalm 92 has been selected, where, among the excluded verses (vv. 5–11), we read, "you have exalted my horn like that of the wild ox; you have poured over me fresh oil" (v. 10). This traditional Sabbath (Saturday) psalm in the weekly Jewish sequence[18] is not long, and the excluded verses are hardly scandalous, even if they are so impolite as to mention the destruction of the wicked and the stupidity of those who have no sense of the works of God. While one could focus solely on the missing verses, the better option would be to simply keep the psalm intact, allowing praise its proper proportion, including the censored verses, but not giving them undue emphasis by making them the focus of a fragmented reading.

Psalm 25, an individual lament, is a confessional acrostic selected for the footwashing scene (25th Ordinary). Although not counted among the seven traditional penitential psalms, it nevertheless, unexpurgated, constitutes the sort of robust confession of which the church today stands in great need. It makes repeated reference to the covenant (vv. 10, 14), shows concern for thoroughgoing forgiveness of all the psalmist's sins (v. 18), seeks the "way(s)" and "paths" of the LORD (vv. 4, 8, 9, 12), and even declares, "he will pluck my feet (!) out of the net" (v. 15).

Psalm 136, the quintessential antiphonal psalm, tells the story of God's work in creation, the exodus, the wilderness, and the conquest of Canaan. Each verse is punctuated with the people's response: "his steadfast love endures for ever!"[19] In light of the New Commandment to love

18. The daily psalms in Judaism are Psalms 24 (Sunday), 48 (Monday), 82 (Tuesday), 94 (Wednesday), 81 (Thursday), 93 (Friday), and 92 (Saturday).

19. I have, however, used this responsive psalm both ways: (1) the leader reads part A

one another as Christ has loved us, there is no more fitting day on which to have the good news of God's love so persistently reiterated.

Psalm 41 is assigned for 27th Ordinary (World Communion Sunday), first, for the reference we have to its theme of betrayal (v. 9) in the Markan (14:18) institutional narrative, a similar reference already occurring in the Johannine narrative (13:18; 25th Ordinary). More positively, the psalm contains assurances of the LORD's healing and sustenance, as well as this eucharistic phrase: "you have . . . set me in your presence forever" (v.12).

For 28th Ordinary, *both* of two short psalms are suggested. Where multiple psalms are generally offered as a choice, here both Psalms 3 and 134 are suggested for use with the scene in Gethsemane. Psalm 134, one of the shortest in the Psalter, is the last of the Psalms of Ascent, suggesting that the psalmist has reached the final stage of his journey; it is also a call to prayer by night. Psalm 3, an individual lament for a nighttime setting, expresses trust in the LORD for deliverance (v. 8), even when the psalmist is evidently ambushed during sleep (vv. 5–7).

Either of Psalms 38 or 55 may be used for 29th Ordinary, in conjunction with the trial before the Sanhedrin. The confessor of Psalm 38, one of the penitential psalms, confesses his sin, but also decries his unjust suffering and declares his trust in the LORD, who sees all; yet the psalmist remains one "in whose mouth is no retort" (v. 14). Psalm 55, also an individual lament, is the prayer of one who has suffered betrayal by an enemy that is sometimes singular, sometimes plural—an enemy, in fact, with whom he has worshipped (v. 13–14).

A fragment of Psalm 33 (vv. 13–22) is assigned to 30th Ordinary when Jesus appears before Pilate, speaking of his otherworldly kingdom (John 18:36). This hymn asserts the LORD's oversight and enthronement over all (vv. 13–15), adding the acute observation: "A king is not saved by his great army" (v. 16; cf. Matt 26:53).

Two other individual laments are suggested for the Lukan road to the cross (31st Ordinary). Psalm 31 is the prayer of one who has become an object of dread, and who sighs, "those who see me in the street flee

---

while the people respond with part B of each verse; (2) the people read part A [NB: this still requires a cue to get the people started], while a leader in a solo voice responds with part B. The advantage of the latter, though slightly more difficult to get off the ground in a decent and orderly way, is that the leader can, in a way that the people as a body cannot, give a variety of inflections to this oft-repeated phrase: "his steadfast love endures forever!"

from me" (v. 11). The unused fragment of Psalm 40 (vv. 12–17), with v. 11 appears to be a self-contained lament, distinct from the song of thanksgiving that precedes it (vv. 1–10).

One can scarcely imagine a more appropriate psalm to attend a reading of the death of Jesus than the unused verses from Psalm 71 (vv. 15–24), in which the psalmist looks back over his life, honors God as his lifelong teacher, and vows that his whole life will proclaim the LORD's wondrous deeds of salvation; even more remarkably, the psalmist expresses the clearest articulation of faith in resurrection: "You who have made me see many troubles and calamities will revive me again; from the depths of the earth you will bring me up again" (v. 20). Most amazing of all is that this psalm would be stripped of these lovely, moving, and comforting verses before finding a place in the *RCL*. They offer a treasured expression of the hope of resurrection concealed in the Old Testament.

Finally, for the burial of Jesus (34th Ordinary), Psalm 77 is a cry of the most desperate grief, even to the point of questioning the very nature of God: "Has his steadfast love ceased for ever? Are his promises at an end for all time?" (v. 8). This is not a psalm for those who "know better," but for those who need permission to vent their deepest despair at the greatest loss, and this is the Sunday to let it all out. It is probably best to use the entire psalm, however, and not merely the omitted verses, for only with the turn to remembrance does the psalm serve its proper function, that is, to convert the sobbing marsh of grief into solid ground for worship, adoration, and praise.

The Old Testament selections are narrower than in previous weeks, thus creating the possibility of treating two minor prophets whose books are entirely (or almost entirely) untouched by the *RCL*, with a third excluded book assigned to Christ the King. For the first week (24th Ordinary), however, Deut 16:1–22 is recommended, as it outlines the three primary festivals that required annual attendance in Jerusalem, including the Passover, for which the disciples are sent to prepare at the end of the gospel reading. On 25th Ordinary, the opening oracle of Isaiah (1:2–9) describes anatomically the sickness of the nation: "From the sole of the foot even to the head, there is no soundness in it" (v. 6). Subsequent (more familiar) verses urge washing and cleansing, promising that scarlet sins will be made like white wool (v. 18), a fitting complement to the *pedilavium*.

With 26th Ordinary, the first of Haggai's five discourses is assigned (1:1–15a), where the returned exiles learn that their individualistic self-concern and neglect of the temple has led to their own hardship. The option of including the second discourse on 27th Ordinary is provided as well, but since this text appears in the *RCL*, 2 Chron 7:1–22 is also suggested, an account of the LORD's response to Solomon's dedication of the temple, in which sacrifices exceed the capacity of the altar, the choir is in full throat, and the priests cannot remain in the temple due to God's palpable glory; after this, Solomon is given this remarkable promise, which cries out for application by the church today: "if my people who are called by my name humble themselves, pray, seek my face, and turn from their wicked ways, then I will hear from heaven, and will forgive their sin and heal their land" (2 Chr 7:14). Although some claim the contextual, historical distance is too great to allow direct application of this text, that empty reasoning could be applied to the entire Bible—and often is! On the contrary, this covenant renewal text is strongly urged here for use at worldwide communion in the spirit of the prayer concerts of old.

The third and fourth addresses of Haggai are assigned to 28th Ordinary, and the fifth to the 29th Ordinary, with no explicit connections to the gospel scenes; nevertheless, the contrasting imagery is evocative in relation to the suffering of Christ in the Garden: before the foundation was laid, all was fruitless; with the foundation will come blessing. Likewise, where Haggai foretells a shaking of heaven and earth that will "overthrow the throne of kingdoms" (2:22), Jesus informs the high priest, "'you will see the Son of Man seated at the right hand of power,' and 'coming with the clouds of heaven'" (Mark 14:62). This quotation from Daniel, of course, lends another option, that is, the expansion of the abridged versions of this vision that appears in the *RCL*. While the omitted verses are beastly and bewildering, the end of the prophecy (7:26–27) is worth the journey; at the very least, it is worth bearing the whole thing in mind, as Daniel did, despite the terror it caused him (7:28).

During the remaining weeks of the Passion (30th–33rd Ordinary), a sequential reading of Nahum unfolds over four weeks. While these oracles against Nineveh may seem an odd choice, their relevance at this juncture is more typological than narrowly historical, and is probably best discerned if the book is read backwards. The enemy whose destruction is forecast here is not the repentant city clothed in sackcloth at Jonah's terse warning, but one that is endlessly cruel (Nah 3:19), whose warring heritage is traceable back to Nimrod himself (Gen 10:8–12). Like Rome, before whose governor Jesus is tried (30th Ordinary), Nineveh is the capital of cruelty for which Jonah was yet "a sign," just as the Son of Man became a sign "to this generation" (Luke 11:30). Briefly, and in the simplest terms, we may perhaps see in typological "Nineveh" that which is defeated in the cosmic battle that the cross represents.

If four weeks of Nahum is too much to bear, alternative selections for the 31st–33rd Sundays of Ordinary Time are suggested from the latter prophets. As Jesus struggles along the road to Calvary (31st Ordinary), Ezekiel 20:32–49 declares God's intention that his people will never be like the nations, but "I will be king over you" and "enter into judgment with you face to face" (vv. 33, 35). At the death of Jesus, an overlooked oracle from Isaiah 48:1–22 rings with messianic overtones (vv. 12, 21), with the new and unheard-of thing (vv. 6–8) the LORD is doing for his own sake (v. 11) and for the sake of his beloved (v. 14). Lastly, Zechariah 12:1—13:1 foretells the coming day of the LORD, when Jerusalem shall mourn as "they look on the one whom they have pierced" (12:10; cf. John 19:34, 37), and a fountain shall open "to cleanse them from sin and impurity" (13:1).

CHRIST THE KING (REIGN OF CHRIST)

John 12:17–19, 37–50 is the gospel lection for Christ the King Sunday, as it is for Christmas Day. Without repeating previous comments on this text concerning God's sovereign *commandment* of eternal life, let it simply be noted that locating this summary of Jesus' ministry here lends a sense of symmetry by way of John's quotation of Isaiah 6:9–10.

The epistle reading is a composite of unused fragments from 1 Cor 15 (vv. 27–34, 39–41), which begins, strikingly, "For God has put all things in subjection under his feet" (v. 27), and ends by distinguishing between various types of glory (vv. 39–41), a distinction with which the gospel is especially concerned (John 12:42–43). In addition to an emphasis on the sovereignty of Christ, which leads to the glorious end that "God will be all in all" (v. 28), the passage includes Paul's description of the Christian life as dying daily to self (v. 31). Admittedly, after the lengthy sojourn through the Passion, the emphasis on resurrection is not as explicit as one might wish to find in this fragmentary reading; for this reason the preacher may wish to consider supplying additional verses from those already included in the RCL. But it is worth mentioning that the foregoing series on the Passion is in no way intended to obscure the weekly festival of the Lord's Day as the day of Resurrection, the "little Easter"; the same is true of every other Sunday in Year D, including Christ the King. We should never preach or pray as though Christ is not already risen, but to gain a sense of God's drama, we also need a healthy sense of incredulity, wonder, and mystery, not in addition to, but as a vital organ of, a living faith.

As with an early pairing of two shorter psalms, both of which were recommended (see 28th Ordinary), here the brief universal call to worship of Psalm 117 is suggested for use, along with Psalm 87, the Song of Zion that announces the LORD's love and favor respecting its "gates" (87:2), and envisions an eschatological registration of the peoples (vv. 5–6). The use of both psalms is especially important here for the sake of maintaining the dialectic of God's universal sovereignty and the particular locus of Jerusalem in God's future. As much as politics, ethics, and interreligious forces have prejudiced the church against interpretations that see a future role for Jerusalem in God's mission, or a legitimate claim to the land for the modern state of Israel, the fact is that such prejudices are without a blessed basis in Scripture. Not that they have no scriptural foundation, but the canon makes it clear that such perspectives are voiced by the enemies of God and of his people: Nineveh, Babylon, Rome, Edom. Yet, Christ remains the missionary of reconciliation, the Prince of Peace. Look again at those who are registered among the peoples and *included* in the song of Zion!

> Among those who know me I mention Rahab and Babylon;
> Philistia too, and Tyre, with Ethiopia—
> "This one was born there," they say. (87:4)

Such a pairing of psalms belongs under what I have termed elsewhere a broad/narrow dialectic,[20] which in this case requires attention to both eschatological expansion and apocalyptic contraction: the "all in all" of the sovereignty of God and the birth pangs that will, reflexively and involuntarily, focus the world's attention on Israel, Jerusalem, and "Zion." Any hermeneutic or ecclesiastical policy that says otherwise is either blind in one eye (Zech 11:17), or built on the shifting sands of biblical illiteracy (Matt 7:26).

Christ the King is also an opportunity to voice another excluded book, the shortest of the Old Testament, and to do so in its entirety in a single reading. Obadiah, like the pairing of the two psalms discussed above, holds in tension the LORD's judgment of a particular nation (Edom) and a vision of God's universal sovereignty (vv. 15, 21). As with

---

20. Slemmons, *Groans of the Spirit*, xv, xx, et al.

Nahum's prophecies against Nineveh, however, understanding the oracle against Edom/Esau requires more than a narrow historical investigation of the circumstances surrounding the book's authorship; it necessitates the intracanonical principle of Scripture interpreting Scripture to understand the thick layers of Edom's spiritual heritage and identity (v. 21). For only in such an investigation will we discover the ambiguity in the prophecy of this judgment, the sense in which Esau/Edom is both traitor (Ps 137:7) and kin (Deut 23:7) to Israel, an ambiguity that fully accords with the ambiguity regarding judgment in the gospel when Jesus declares that his mission is not to judge, but that there will be a judgment: "the word that I have spoken will serve as judge" (John 12:48). In light of such a tension, the preacher of Year D texts will do well to preach accordingly: never as judge, but seeing to it that the Word of the LORD is clearly and plainly stated, that the Word itself will do its work.

ALL SAINTS'

For All Saints' Day (November 1), the gospel focuses on unique Matthean material (27:52–53) that refers to the general resurrection of many saints who vacated their tombs after Jesus rose from the dead. It also includes the description of the women who watched the final events of his Passion (27:55–56). For the sake of coherence, a broader reading should include, at a minimum, the entire sequence from 27:50–61.

Third John is suggested for the epistle reading. This otherwise silent epistle probably deserves a more prominent place than All Saints' Day, for it has important things to say about the need to support missionaries and evangelists, and to forego support from the world (vv. 5–8). Yet its message accords with the identity and vocation of the church, so let its message go forth!

The Psalm reading consists of fragments from Psalm 107 (vv. 10–16, 38–42), which reflect the testimony of those who have experienced the redemptive liberation of God, but which would also benefit by retaining the introduction (vv. 1–3), more of the closing hymn (vv. 33–37), and the conclusion (v. 43).

Lastly, the first oracle of Haggai (1:1–15a) is given another opportunity here (see 26th Ordinary), as is 2 Chronicles 19:4—20:30, a wonderful, overlooked text from the reign of Jehoshaphat, in which the LORD wins a mighty (defensive) victory for Judah (20:17) while the people simply sing (20:20–23). This too is a text that deserves a hearing in the Sunday rotation, yet its doxological themes clearly resonate with the eschatological worship of God by the saints in heaven—thus its placement on this festival that will only occasionally fall on the LORD's Day.

Appendix A
Year D—Texts for Preaching

THE ADVENT–CHRISTMAS–EPIPHANY CYCLE

First Sunday of Advent	Mal 1:1–14 Psalm 18 Luke 1:1–25 Heb 1:13—2:4
Second Sunday of Advent	Num 12:1–16 OR 20:1–13 (14–21) 22–29 Ps 106:(1) 7–18, 24–28 (43–48) (OR Psalm 95) Luke 1:(57) 58–67 (68–79) 80 Heb 3:1–19
Third Sunday of Advent	Josh 23:1–16 Ps 81:(1) 2–9 (10–16) (OR Psalm 95) Luke 3:23–38 OR Matt 1:1–17 Heb 4:1–11 (12–16)
Fourth Sunday of Advent	Num 14:1–25 Psalm 144 John 3:22–38 Heb 5:11—6:20
Christmas Eve (Proper I)	Eccl 5:1–20 OR 7:1–14 OR Ezek 33:23–33 Psalm 21 Matt 12:22–50 OR Luke 11:14–54 Phil 3:1–4a; 4:10–21 (OR Jas 1:17–27)
Christmas Morning (Proper II)	Eccl 7:15–29 OR Mic 7:1–20 Psalm 44 Matt 10:9–23 OR Luke 12:1–12 Rom 3:1–22a

Christmas Day (Proper III)	Isa 6:(8) 9–13 OR Jer 10:1–16 (17–25) Psalm 35 OR Psalm 94 John 12:17–19, 37–50 Rom 11:2b–28 (29–32) 33–36
First Sunday of Christmas	Gen 14:1–24 Psalm 110 Matt 8:14–34 OR Mark 5:1–20 Heb 7:1–28
Second Sunday of Christmas	Exod 25:1–40 Ps 73 Matt 11:1 (2–11) 12–15 (16–19) 20–24 (25–30) OR Luke 7:18–35 Heb 8:1–13
Epiphany (January 6)	Deut 4:(9) 10–24 (25–31) 32–40 Psalm 75 OR Psalm 76 John 5:31–47 1 John 2:3–29
Baptism of the LORD (First Sunday in Ordinary Time)	Lev 16:1–34 Psalm 69 Matt 14:1–12 Heb 9:1–28
Second Sunday in Ordinary Time	Isa 26:7—27:1 Psalm 109 Matt 8:1–4; 9:1–8 OR Luke 5:12–26 Heb 10:1–4 (10–14) 26–39
Third Sunday in Ordinary Time	Job 32:1–22 Ps 89:5–18, 38–52 Luke 5:27–39 Heb 11:(1–3) 4–7, 17–28 (39–40)
Fourth Sunday in Ordinary Time*	Job 33:1–33 Ps 34:11–18 Matt 12:1–21 OR Mark 3:7–19 OR Luke 6:1–16 Heb 12:(1–3) 4–17
Fifth Sunday in Ordinary Time*	Job 34:1–20 Psalm 28 Matt 6:7–15 Heb 13:9–14 (15–16) 17–25
Sixth Sunday in Ordinary Time* [Proper 1]	Job 34:21–37 Psalm 12 Matt 7:1–12 2 Pet 1:1–15

Seventh Sunday in Ordinary Time* [Proper 2]	Job 35:1–16 Ps 119:(1–16) 17–32 Matt 7:13–20 2 Pet 2:1–22
Eighth Sunday in Ordinary Time* [Proper 3]	Job 36:1–23 Psalm 61 Matt 13:53–58 2 Pet 3:1–7 (8–14) 15–18
Transfiguration Sunday	Job 36:24—37:24 Psalm 11 Matt 8:5–13 OR John 4:43–54 Jude 1–25 (OR Heb 13:9–14, 17–25, if Transfiguration preempts the Fifth Sunday of Ordinary Time)

[* = Fourth to Eighth Sundays in Ordinary Time may be preempted by Transfiguration Sunday]

THE LENT–RESURRECTION–PENTECOST CYCLE

Ash Wednesday	Isa 57:1–21 Psalm 102 John 5:1–18 Jas 1:1–16 OR Eph 2:11–22 (OR Gal 1:1–24)
First Sunday of Lent	Deut 10:12–22 OR Neh 9:1–38 Psalm 6 John 7:1–13 Gal 2:1–14(15–21) (OR 1:1–24) OR Jas 1:1–16 (17–27) OR (1:17—2:10) 2:11–13
Second Sunday of Lent	Ezek 47:1–12 Psalm 143 John 7:14–36 (37–39) Jas 2:(14–17)18–26 OR 2:(1–10) 11–13(14–17) 18–26 OR Gal 2:1–14(15–21)
Third Sunday of Lent	Gen 13:1–18 OR 2 Sam 7:18–29 Psalm 38 John 7:40–52 Gal 3:1–22 (23–29) (OR Jas 3:1–18)
Fourth Sunday of Lent	Isa 54:1–17 OR 37:14–38 Psalm 39 John 8:12–30 Jas 4:(1–3) 4–6 (7–8a) 8b–17 OR Gal 4:1–3 (4–7) 8–31 (5:1)

Fifth Sunday of Lent	Gen 4:1–16 OR Isa 63:(7–9) 10–19 Psalm 101 John 8:31–47 Gal 5:(1)2–12 (13–25) 26 OR Jas 5:1–6(7–10)11–12(13–20)
Sixth Sunday of Lent (Palm Sunday)	Deut 11:1–17 OR Isa 43:8–15 Psalm 94 OR Psalm 35 John 8:48–59 Rom 1:8–15 (16–17) 18–32; 2:1–11 OR Gal 6:1–6(7–16)17–18
Maundy Thursday	Deut 30:1–14 Psalm 115 (OR Psalm 113) John 7:53—8:11 OR Luke 22:1–38 (39–46) Rom 2:12–29
Good Friday	Ezra 9:5–15 OR Jer 25:15–38 OR 2 Chr 7:1–22 Psalm 88 Luke 23:(1–12) 13–49 1 Pet 4:(1–8) 9–11 (12–14) 15–19
Holy Saturday (Great Vigil)	Num 10:33–36; Deut 10:11—12:1; Judg 5:1–31; Song 4:9—5:16; Isa 26:1–21 Psalmss 7; 17; 44; 57 OR 108; 119:145–76; 149 Matt 7:1–23; Luke 7:36—8:3; Matt 27:62–66 1 Cor 15:27–34 (35–38) 39–41 (42–58)
Resurrection of the LORD	Deut 7:1–26 Ps 71:15–24 OR Ps 75 OR Ps 76 John 5:19–30 2 Cor 1:1–17 (18–22) OR Phil 1:1–2 (3–11) 12–20
Resurrection Evening	Exod 34:27–28 (29–35) OR Deut 9:8–21 Ps 71:15–24 OR Psalm 75 OR Psalm 76 John 21:20–25 (OR Luke 24:36–49 OR John 20:19–31) 2 Cor 3:7–11(4:16—5:1)5:2–5(6–10) OR Rev 1:1–3 (4–8) 9–20
2nd Sunday of Easter	Hos 14:1–9 Ps 64 OR Ps 119:73–96 John 16:16–24 2 Cor 1:23—2:17
3rd Sunday of Easter	Zech 13:1–9 Psalm 60 OR Psalm 108 John 16:25–33 2 Cor 6:11—7:1
4th Sunday of Easter	Gen 38:1–30 OR Eccl 5:1–20 Psalm 10 Matt 22:23–33 OR Mark 12:18–27 AND Luke 20:39–40 2 Cor 7:2–16

5th Sunday of Easter	1 Sam 21:1–15 OR 2 Kgs 4:38–44 Ps 49:(1–12) 13–20 Matt 15:29–39; 16:1–12 OR Mark 8:1–26 2 Cor 8:1–6 (7–15) 16–24
6th Sunday of Easter	Deut 15:1–18 OR 19:15–21 Psalm 129 Matt 18:1–14 (15–20) OR Luke 9:46–50; 17:1–4 2 Cor 9:1–15
Ascension (Thursday)	Prov 1:1–7 Ps 119:145–76 Mark 12:35–37 OR Luke 20:41–47 1 John 2:3–29
7th Sunday of Easter	Jer 9:23–24; 24:1–10 Psalm 115 Mark 11:27–33 (AND Mark 12:35–37, if Ascension not observed) OR Luke 20:1–8 (AND Luke 20:41–47, if Ascension not observed) OR John 21:20–25 2 Cor 10:1–17
Pentecost Sunday	Exod 4:1–17 OR Deut 5:1–33 OR 31:23–29 OR Dan 12:1–13 Ps 119:113–36 Matt 10:9–23 OR Luke 12:1–12 2 Cor 11:1—12:1

TRINITY–ORDINARY TIME–CHRIST THE KING

Trinity Sunday	1 Kgs 9:1–9; 11:1–13 OR Eccl 8:1–17 Psalm 35 John 15:18–25 (26–27); 16:1–4a 2 Cor 12:11–21; 13:1–10 (11–13)
9th Sunday in Ordinary Time [Proper 4]	Deut 31:30—32:27 OR Isa 5:8–17 Psalm 142 Matt 17:9–20 OR Mark 9:9–29 OR Luke 9:18–27 (28–36) 37–45 Phil 2:14–30
10th Sunday in Ordinary Time [Proper 5]	Deut 32:28–47 OR Isa 5:18–30 Psalm 74 Matt 12:22–37 OR Luke 11:14–23 1 John 3:8–15 (16–24); 4:1–6
11th Sunday in Ordinary Time [Proper 6]	Isa 6:(8) 9–13 OR Ezek 17:22–24 OR 31:1–18 OR Dan 4:1–37 Psalm 7 Matt 13:10–17 (18–33) 34–35 OR Mark 4:1–25 OR Luke 8:4–25; 13:18–21 Eph 4:17–24 (26–32; 5:1–2) 3–7 OR 2 Pet 2:1–22

12th Sunday in Ordinary Time [Proper 7]	Isa 29:1–24 OR 59:1–21 Psalm 55 Matt 15:1–20 OR Mark 7:1–20 1 Tim 4:1–16
13th Sunday in Ordinary Time [Proper 8]	2 Kgs 20:1–21 OR Amos 4:1–13 OR Mal 3:5–18; 4: (1–2a) 2b–6 Psalm 56 Matt 9:27–34 OR John 5:31–47 1 Cor 3:12–15 (3:16—4:5) 4:6–21 OR 2 John 1–13
14th Sunday in Ordinary Time [Proper 9]	2 Kgs 6:8–23 Psalm 57 OR Psalm 3 Matt 12:38–50 OR Luke 11:24–36 1 Cor 5:1–6a (6b–8) 9–13; 6:1–11

THE APOCALYPTIC DISCOURSE
[15th–19th Sundays in Ordinary Time]

15th Sunday in Ordinary Time [Proper 10]	Jer 7:1–15 OR Dan 2:1–49 Ps 17:8–14 (15) OR Psalm 83 Matt 24:1–8 (OR Mark 13:1–8) 1 Cor 7:1–40
16th Sunday in Ordinary Time [Proper 11]	Deut 31:23–29 OR Mic 7:1–7 OR Dan (11:40–45) 12:1–13 Psalm 54 Matt 10:17–22a; 24:9–14 OR Mark 13:9–13 1 Cor 9:1–15
17th Sunday in Ordinary Time [Proper 12]	Deut 4:32–40 OR Isa 65:10–16 (17–25) OR Ezek 7:(1–9) 10–27 OR Zech 14:(1–3) 4–9 (10–21) Ps 50:(7–8) 9–21 (22–23) OR 105:(1–6) 12–15 (26) 27–36 (37, 43–45) Matt 24:15–22 OR Mark 13:14–20 OR Luke 21:20–24 1 Cor 10:(14–17) 18—11:1
18th Sunday in Ordinary Time [Proper 13]	Gen 19:1–29 Psalm 59 Matt 24:23–35 (36–44) OR Luke 17:20–37 1 John 2:3–29 OR 2 John 1–13 OR 2 Pet 2:1–22
19th Sunday in Ordinary Time [Proper 14]	Gen 6:1–8 OR Zech 9:1–8 (9–10) 11–17 Ps 37:(1–2) 12–38 (39–40) Matt 24:(36–44) 45–51 OR Luke 12:(35–40) 41–48 1 Cor 11:2–22 (23–26) 27–34

PRELUDE TO THE PASSION

[20th–23rd Sundays in Ordinary Time]

20th Sunday in Ordinary Time [Proper 15]	Jer 22:1–9 OR Zech 7:1–14 Psalm 58 Matt 23:13–39 OR Luke 11:37–54 1 Tim 3:1–16
21st Sunday in Ordinary Time [Proper 16]	Gen 3:1–7 (8–15) 16–24 OR Jer 8:4–13 OR 24:1–10 OR Hab 3:1–19 Psalm 140 Matt 21:12–22 OR Mark 11:12–25 (26) Col 1:29—2:5 (16–19) 20–23
22nd Sunday in Ordinary Time [Proper 17]	Num 11:1–30 OR Isa 45:14–25 OR Jer 4:19–31 OR Zech 8:1–23 Ps 68:11–31 (32–35) OR Psalm 120 (OR Psalm 82) John 10:19–21 (22–30) 31–42 1 Cor 14:1–40
23rd Sunday in Ordinary Time [Proper 18]	Exod 28:15–30 OR 2 Sam 15:30–37; 16:15–19, 23; 17:1–23 OR 2 Chr 30:1–27 Psalm 141 John 11:(45) 46–57 1 Cor 16:1–24

THE PASSION OF OUR LORD JESUS CHRIST

[24th–33rd Sundays in Ordinary Time]

24th Sunday in Ordinary Time [Proper 19]	Deut 16:1–22 Ps 92: (1–4) 5–11 (12–15) Matt 26:1–19 OR Mark 14:1–16 OR Luke 22:1–13 1 Tim 5:1–23
25th Sunday in Ordinary Time [Proper 20]	Isa 1:(1) 2–9 (10–20) Ps 25:11–22 John 13:(1–17) 18–20 Titus 1:1–16
26th Sunday in Ordinary Time [Proper 21]	Hag 1:1–15a Psalm 136 John 13:21–38 Eph 5:21–33; 6:1–9 (10–20) 21–24

27th Sunday in Ordinary Time (World Communion) [Proper 22]	2 Chr 7:1–22 (OR Hag 1:15b—2:9) Psalm 41 Matt 26:20–35 OR Mark 14:17–31 OR Luke 22:14–38 Col 3:18—4:18 OR 1 Pet 2:1, 11–18 (19–25); 3:1–12
29th Sunday in Ordinary Time [Proper 24]	Hag 2:20–23 OR Dan 7:(1–3) 4–8 (9–18) 19–28 Psalm 38 OR Psalm 55 Matt 26:57—27:2 OR Mark 14:53—15:1 OR Luke 22:54—23:1 OR John 18:13–28 Rom 9:6–33
30th Sunday in Ordinary Time [Proper 25]	Nah 1:1–8 Ps 33: (1–12) 13–22 Matt 27:3–31a OR Mark 15:2–20a OR Luke 23:2–25 OR John 18:29—19:16 Rom 10:1–4, 16–21 OR 11:2b–28 (29–32) 33–36
31st Sunday in Ordinary Time [Proper 26]	Nah 1:9–15 OR Ezek 20:32–49 Ps 31:(1–5)6–14(15–16) 17–24 OR Ps 40:(1–11)12–17 Luke 23:26–32 Rom 15:1–3, 14–33
32nd Sunday in Ordinary Time [Proper 27]	Nah 2:1–13 OR Isa 48:1–22 Ps 71:15–24 Matt 27:31b–56 OR Mark 15:20b–41 OR Luke 23:33–49 OR John 19:17–30 Rom 13:1–7; 14:13–23
33rd Sunday in Ordinary Time [Proper 28]	Nah 3:1–19 OR Zech 12:1–13:1 Ps 77:(1–2) 3–10 (11–20) Matt 27:57–66 OR Mark 15:42–47 OR Luke 23:50–56 OR John 19:31–42 Rom 16:1–25 (26–27) OR Phil 3:1–4a; 4:10–23
Christ the King/Reign of Christ (34th in Ordinary Time) [Proper 29]	Obad 1–21 Psalms 87 AND 117 John 12:17–19, 37–50 1 Cor 15:27–34 (35–38) 39–41 (42–58)
All Saints' Day (November 1)	Hag 1:1–15a OR 2 Chr 19:4—20:30 Ps 107: (1–3) 10–16 (23–37) 38–42 (43) Matt 27:(45–49) 50–56 (57–61) 3 John 1–15

Appendix B
Year D—Scripture Index of Lections

Gen 3:1–7 (8–15) 16–24	21st Sunday in Ordinary Time
Gen 4:1–16	Fifth Sunday of Lent
Gen 6:1–8	19th Sunday in Ordinary Time
Gen 13:1–18	Third Sunday of Lent
Gen 14:1–24	First Sunday of Christmas
Gen 19:1–29	18th Sunday in Ordinary Time
Gen 38:1–30	4th Sunday of Easter
Exod 4:1–17	Pentecost Sunday
Exod 25:1–40	Second Sunday of Christmas
Exod 28:15–30	23rd Sunday in Ordinary Time
Exod 34:27–28 (29–35)	Resurrection Evening
Lev 16:1–34	Baptism of the LORD (First Ordinary)
Num 10:33–36	Holy Saturday (Great Vigil)
Num 11:1–30	22nd Sunday in Ordinary Time
Num 12:1–16	Second Sunday of Advent
Num 14:1–25	Fourth Sunday of Advent
Num 20:1–13 (14–21) 22–29	Second Sunday of Advent
Deut 4:(9) 10–24 (25–31) 32–40	Epiphany (January 6)

Deut 4:32–40	17th Sunday in Ordinary Time
Deut 5:1–33	Pentecost Sunday
Deut 7:1–26	Resurrection of the LORD
Deut 9:8–21	Resurrection Evening
Deut 10:11—12:1	Holy Saturday (Great Vigil)
Deut 10:12–22	First Sunday of Lent
Deut 11:1–17	Sixth Sunday of Lent (Palm)
Deut 15:1–18	6th Sunday of Easter
Deut 16:1–22	24th Sunday in Ordinary Time
Deut 19:15–21	6th Sunday of Easter
Deut 30:1–14	Maundy Thursday
Deut 31:23–29	Pentecost Sunday
Deut 31:(1–22) 23–29	16th Sunday in Ordinary Time
Deut 31:30—32:27	9th Sunday in Ordinary Time
Deut 32:28–47	10th Sunday in Ordinary Time
Josh 23:1–16	Third Sunday of Advent
Judg 5:1–31	Holy Saturday (The Great Vigil)
1 Sam 21:1–15	5th Sunday of Easter
2 Sam 7:18–29	Third Sunday of Lent
2 Sam 15:30–37; 16:15–19, 23; 17:1–23	23rd Sunday in Ordinary Time
1 Kgs 9:1–9; 11:1–13	Trinity Sunday
2 Kgs 4:38–44	5th Sunday of Easter
2 Kgs 6:8–23	14th Sunday in Ordinary Time
2 Kgs 20:1–21	13th Sunday in Ordinary Time
2 Chr 7:1–22	Good Friday
2 Chr 7:1–22	27th Ordinary (World Communion)

2 Chr 19:4—20:30	All Saints' Day
2 Chr 30:1–27	23rd Sunday in Ordinary Time
Ezra 9:5–15	Good Friday
Neh 9:1–38	First Sunday of Lent
Job 32:1–22	Third Sunday in Ordinary Time
Job 33:1–33	Fourth Sunday in Ordinary Time
Job 34:1–20	Fifth Sunday in Ordinary Time
Job 34:21–37	Sixth Sunday in Ordinary Time
Job 35:1–16	Seventh Sunday in Ordinary Time
Job 36:1–23	Eighth Sunday in Ordinary Time
Job 36:24—37:24	Transfiguration Sunday
Psalm 3	14th Sunday in Ordinary Time
Psalm 3	28th Sunday in Ordinary Time
Psalm 6	First Sunday of Lent
Psalm 7	Holy Saturday (Great Vigil)
Ps 7	11th Sunday in Ordinary Time
Psalm 10	4th Sunday of Easter
Psalm 11	Transfiguration Sunday
Psalm 12	Sixth Sunday in Ordinary Time
Psalm 17	Holy Saturday (Great Vigil)
Ps 17:8–14 (15)	15th Sunday in Ordinary Time
Psalm 18	First Sunday of Advent
Psalm 21	Christmas Eve (Proper I)
Ps 25:11–22	25th Sunday in Ordinary Time
Ps 28	Fifth Sunday in Ordinary Time
Ps 31:(1–5) 6–14 (15–16) 17–24	31st Sunday in Ordinary Time
Ps 33:(1–12) 13–22	30th Sunday in Ordinary Time
Ps 34:11–18	Fourth Sunday in Ordinary Time
Psalm 35	Christmas Day (Proper III)

Psalm 35	Sixth Sunday of Lent (Palm)
Psalm 35	Trinity Sunday
Ps 37:(1–2) 12–38 (39–40)	19th Sunday in Ordinary Time
Psalm 38	Third Sunday of Lent
Psalm 38	29th Sunday in Ordinary Time
Psalm 39	Fourth Sunday of Lent
Ps 40:(1–11) 12–17	31st Sunday in Ordinary Time
Psalm 41	27th Ordinary (World Communion)
Psalm 44	Christmas Morning (Proper II)
Psalm 44	Holy Saturday (Great Vigil)
Ps 49:(1–12) 13–20	5th Sunday of Easter
Ps 50:(7–8) 9–21 (22–23)	17th Sunday in Ordinary Time
Psalm 54	16th Sunday in Ordinary Time
Psalm 55	12th Sunday in Ordinary Time
Psalm 55	29th Sunday in Ordinary Time
Psalm 56	13th Sunday in Ordinary Time
Psalm 57	Holy Saturday (Great Vigil)
Psalm 57	14th Sunday in Ordinary Time
Psalm 58	20th Sunday in Ordinary Time
Psalm 59	18th Sunday in Ordinary Time
Psalm 60	3rd Sunday of Easter
Psalm 61	Eighth Sunday in Ordinary Time
Psalm 64	2nd Sunday of Easter
Ps 68:11–31 (32–35)	22nd Sunday in Ordinary Time
Psalm 69	Baptism of the LORD (First Ordinary)
Ps 71:15–24	Resurrection of the LORD
Ps 71:15–24	Resurrection Evening
Ps 71:15–24	32nd Sunday in Ordinary Time
Psalm 73	Second Sunday of Christmas
Psalm 74	10th Sunday in Ordinary Time
Psalm 75	Epiphany (January 6)
Psalm 75	Resurrection of the LORD
Psalm 75	Resurrection Evening

Psalm 76	Epiphany (January 6)
Psalm 76	Resurrection of the LORD
Psalm 76	Resurrection Evening
Ps 77:(1–2) 3–10 (11–20)	33rd Sunday in Ordinary Time
Ps 81:(1) 2–9 (10–16)	Third Sunday of Advent
Psalm 82	22nd Sunday in Ordinary Time
Psalm 87	Christ the King
Psalm 88	Good Friday
Ps 89:5–18, 38–52	Third Sunday in Ordinary Time
Ps 92:(1–4) 5–11 (12–15)	24th Sunday in Ordinary Time
Psalm 94	Christmas Day (Proper III)
Psalm 94	Sixth Sunday of Lent (Palm)
Psalm (95)	Second Sunday of Advent
Psalm (95)	Third Sunday of Advent
Psalm 101	Fifth Sunday of Lent
Psalm 102	Ash Wednesday
Ps 105:(1–6) 2–15, 26–36 (37, 43–45)	17th Sunday in Ordinary Time
Ps 106:(1) 7–18, 24–28 (43–48)	Second Sunday of Advent
Ps 107:(1–3) 10–16 (23–37) 38–42 (43)	All Saints' Day
Psalm 108	Holy Saturday (Great Vigil)
Psalm 108	3rd Sunday of Easter
Psalm 109	Second Sunday in Ordinary Time
Psalm 110	First Sunday of Christmas
Psalm 113	Maundy Thursday
Psalm 115	Maundy Thursday
Psalm 115	7th Sunday of Easter
Psalm 117	Christ the King
Ps 119:(1–16) 17–32	Seventh Sunday in Ordinary Time
Ps 119:73–96	2nd Sunday of Easter
Ps 119:113–136	Pentecost Sunday
Ps 119:145–176	Holy Saturday (Great Vigil)
Ps 119:145–176	Ascension (Thursday)
Psalm 129	6th Sunday of Easter

Psalm 134	28th Sunday in Ordinary Time
Psalm 136	26th Sunday in Ordinary Time
Psalm 140	21st Sunday in Ordinary Time
Psalm 141	23rd Sunday in Ordinary Time
Psalm 142	9th Sunday in Ordinary Time
Psalm 143	Second Sunday of Lent
Psalm 144	Fourth Sunday of Advent
Psalm 149	Holy Saturday (Great Vigil)
Prov 1:1–7	Ascension (Thursday)
Eccl 5:1–20	Christmas Eve (Proper I)
Eccl 5:1–20	4th Sunday of Easter
Eccl 7:1–14	Christmas Eve (Proper I)
Eccl 7:15–29	Christmas Morning (Proper II)
Eccl 8:1–17	Trinity Sunday
Song 4:9—5:16	Holy Saturday (Great Vigil)
Isa 1:(1) 2–9 (10–20)	25th Sunday in Ordinary Time
Isa 5:8–17	9th Sunday in Ordinary Time
Isa 5:18–30	10th Sunday in Ordinary Time
Isa 6:(8) 9–13	Christmas Day (Proper III)
Isa 6:(8) 9–13	11th Sunday in Ordinary Time
Isa 26:1–21	Holy Saturday (Great Vigil)
Isa 26:7–27:1	Second Sunday in Ordinary Time
Isa 29:1–24	12th Sunday in Ordinary Time
Isa 37:14–38	Fourth Sunday of Lent
Isa 43:8–15	Sixth Sunday of Lent (Palm)
Isa 45:14–25	22nd Sunday in Ordinary Time
Isa 48:1–22	32nd Sunday in Ordinary Time
Isa 54:1–17	Fourth Sunday of Lent
Isa 57:14–21	Ash Wednesday

Isa 63:(7–9) 10–19	Fifth Sunday of Lent
Isa 65:10–16 (17–25)	17th Sunday in Ordinary Time
Jer 4:19–31	22nd Sunday in Ordinary Time
Jer 7:1–15	15th Sunday in Ordinary Time
Jer 8:4–13	21st Sunday in Ordinary Time
Jer 9:23–24; 24:1–10	7th Sunday of Easter
Jer 10:1–16 (17–25)	Christmas Day (Proper III)
Jer 22:1–9	20th Sunday in Ordinary Time
Jer 24:1–10	21st Sunday in Ordinary Time
Jer 25:15–38	Good Friday
Ezek 7:(1–9) 10–27	17th Sunday in Ordinary Time
Ezek 17:22–24	11th Sunday in Ordinary Time
Ezek 20:32–49	31st Sunday in Ordinary Time
Ezek 31:1–18	11th Sunday in Ordinary Time
Ezek 33:23–33	Christmas Eve (Proper I)
Ezek 47:1–12	Second Sunday of Lent
Dan 2:1–49	15th Sunday in Ordinary Time
Dan 4:1–37	11th Sunday in Ordinary Time
Dan 7:(1–3) 4–8 (9–18) 19–28	29th Sunday in Ordinary Time
Dan (11:40–45) 12:1–13	16th Sunday in Ordinary Time
Dan 12:1–13	Pentecost Sunday
Hos 14:1–9	2nd Sunday of Easter
Amos 4:1–13	13th Sunday in Ordinary Time
Obad 1–21	Christ the King
Mic 7:1–7	16th Sunday in Ordinary Time
Mic 7:1–20	Christmas Morning (Proper II)

Nah 1:1–8	30th Sunday in Ordinary Time
Nah 1:9–15	31st Sunday in Ordinary Time
Nah 2:1–13	32nd Sunday in Ordinary Time
Nah 3:1–19	33rd Sunday in Ordinary Time
Hab 3:1–19	21st Sunday in Ordinary Time
Hag 1:1–15a	26th Sunday in Ordinary Time
Hag 1:1–15a	All Saints' Day
Hag (1:15b—2:9)	27th Ordinary (World Communion)
Hag 2:10–19	28th Sunday in Ordinary Time
Hag 2:20–23	29th Sunday in Ordinary Time
Zech 7:1–14	20th Sunday in Ordinary Time
Zech 8:1–23	22nd Sunday in Ordinary Time
Zech 9:1–8 (9–12) 13–17	19th Sunday in Ordinary Time
Zech 12:1—13:1	33rd Sunday in Ordinary Time
Zech 13:1–9	3rd Sunday of Easter
Zech 14:(1–3) 4–9 (10–21)	17th Sunday in Ordinary Time
Mal 1:1–14	First Sunday of Advent
Mal 3:5–18; 4:(1–2a) 2b–6	13th Sunday in Ordinary Time
Matt 1:1–17	Third Sunday of Advent
Matt 6:7–15	Fifth Sunday in Ordinary Time
Matt 7:1–23	Holy Saturday (Great Vigil)
Matt 7:1–12	Sixth Sunday in Ordinary Time
Matt 7:13–20	Seventh Sunday in Ordinary Time
Matt 8:1–4; 9:1–8	Second Sunday in Ordinary Time
Matt 8:5–13	Transfiguration Sunday
Matt 8:14–34	First Sunday of Christmas
Matt 9:27–34	13th Sunday in Ordinary Time
Matt 10:9–23	Christmas Morning (Proper II)

Matt 10:9–23	Pentecost Sunday
Matt 10:17–22a; 24:9–14	16th Sunday in Ordinary Time
Matt 11:1 (2–11) 12–15 (16–19) 20–24 (25–30)	Second Sunday of Christmas
Matt 12:1–21	Fourth Sunday in Ordinary Time
Matt 12:22–50	Christmas Eve (Proper I)
Matt 12:22–37	10th Sunday in Ordinary Time
Matt 12:38–50	14th Sunday in Ordinary Time
Matt 13:10–17 (18–33) 34–35	11th Sunday in Ordinary Time
Matt 13:53–58	Eighth Sunday in Ordinary Time
Matt 14:1–12	Baptism of the LORD (First Ordinary)
Matt 15:1–20	12th Sunday in Ordinary Time
Matt 15:29–39; 16:1–12	5th Sunday of Easter
Matt 17:9–20	9th Sunday in Ordinary Time
Matt 18:1–14 (15–20)	6th Sunday of Easter
Matt 21:12–22	21st Sunday in Ordinary Time
Matt 22:23–33	4th Sunday of Easter
Matt 23:13–39	20th Sunday in Ordinary Time
Matt 24:1–8	15th Sunday in Ordinary Time
Matt 24:15–22	17th Sunday in Ordinary Time
Matt 24:23–35 (36–44)	18th Sunday in Ordinary Time
Matt 24:(36–44) 45–51	19th Sunday in Ordinary Time
Matt 26:1–19	24th Sunday in Ordinary Time
Matt 26:20–35	27th Ordinary (World Communion)
Matt 26:36–56	28th Sunday in Ordinary Time
Matt 26:57—27:2	29th Sunday in Ordinary Time
Matt 27:3–31a	30th Sunday in Ordinary Time
Matt 27:31b–56	32nd Sunday in Ordinary Time
Matt 27:(45–49) 50–56 (57–61)	All Saints' Day
Matt 27:57–66	33rd Sunday in Ordinary Time
Matt 27:62–66	Holy Saturday (Great Vigil)
Mark 3:7–19	Fourth Sunday in Ordinary Time
Mark 4:1–25	11th Sunday in Ordinary Time

Mark 5:1–20	First Sunday of Christmas
Mark 7:1–20	12th Sunday in Ordinary Time
Mark 8:1–26	5th Sunday of Easter
Mark 9:9–29	9th Sunday in Ordinary Time
Mark 11:12–25 (26)	21st Sunday in Ordinary Time
Mark 11:27–33	7th Sunday of Easter
Mark 12:18–27	4th Sunday of Easter
Mark 12:35–37	Ascension (Thursday)
Mark 12:35–37	7th Sunday of Easter
Mark (13:1–8)	15th Sunday in Ordinary Time
Mark 13:9–13	16th Sunday in Ordinary Time
Mark 13:14–23	17th Sunday in Ordinary Time
Mark 14:1–16	24th Sunday in Ordinary Time
Mark 14:17–31	27th Ordinary (World Communion)
Mark 14:32–52	28th Sunday in Ordinary Time
Mark 14:53—15:1	29th Sunday in Ordinary Time
Mark 15:2–20a	30th Sunday in Ordinary Time
Mark 15:20b–41	32nd Sunday in Ordinary Time
Mark 15:42–47	33rd Sunday in Ordinary Time
Luke 1:1–25	First Sunday of Advent
Luke 1:(57) 58–67 (68–79) 80	Second Sunday of Advent
Luke 3:23–38	Third Sunday of Advent
Luke 5:12–26	Second Sunday in Ordinary Time
Luke 5:27–39	Third Sunday in Ordinary Time
Luke 6:1–16	Fourth Sunday in Ordinary Time
Luke 7:18–35	Second Sunday of Christmas
Luke 7:36—8:3	Holy Saturday (Great Vigil)
Luke 8:4–25; 13:18–21	11th Sunday in Ordinary Time
Luke 9:18–27 (28–36) 37–45	9th Sunday in Ordinary Time
Luke 9:46–50; 17:1–4	6th Sunday of Easter
Luke 11:14–54	Christmas Eve (Proper I)
Luke 11:14–23	10th Sunday in Ordinary Time

Luke 11:24–36	14th Sunday in Ordinary Time
Luke 11:37–54	20th Sunday in Ordinary Time
Luke 12:(35–40) 41–48	19th Sunday in Ordinary Time
Luke 12:1–12	Christmas Morning (Proper II)
Luke 12:1–12	Pentecost Sunday
Luke 17:20–37	18th Sunday in Ordinary Time
Luke 20:1–8	7th Sunday of Easter
Luke 20:39–40	4th Sunday of Easter
Luke 20:41–47	Ascension (Thursday)
Luke 20:41–47	7th Sunday of Easter
Luke 21:20–24	17th Sunday in Ordinary Time
Luke 22:1–38 (39–46)	Maundy Thursday
Luke 22:1–13	24th Sunday in Ordinary Time
Luke 22:14–38	27th Ordinary (World Communion)
Luke 22:39–53	28th Sunday in Ordinary Time
Luke 22:54—23:1	29th Sunday in Ordinary Time
Luke 23:(1–12) 13–49	Good Friday
Luke 23:2–25	30th Sunday in Ordinary Time
Luke 23:26–32	31st Sunday in Ordinary Time
Luke 23:33–49	32nd Sunday in Ordinary Time
Luke 23:50–56	33rd Sunday in Ordinary Time
Luke (24:36–49)	Resurrection Evening
John 3:22–38	Fourth Sunday of Advent
John 4:43–54	Transfiguration Sunday
John 5:1–18	Ash Wednesday
John 5:19–30	Resurrection of the LORD
John 5:31–47	Epiphany (January 6)
John 5:31–47	13th Sunday in Ordinary Time
John 7:1–13	First Sunday of Lent
John 7:14–36 (37–39)	Second Sunday of Lent
John 7:40–52	Third Sunday of Lent
John 7:53—8:11	Maundy Thursday

John 8:12–30	Fourth Sunday of Lent
John 8:31–47	Fifth Sunday of Lent
John 8:48–59	Sixth Sunday of Lent (Palm)
John 10:19–21 (22–30) 31–42	22nd Sunday in Ordinary Time
John 11:(45) 46–57	23rd Sunday in Ordinary Time
John 12:17–19, 37–50	Christmas Day (Proper III)
John 12:17–19, 37–50	Christ the King
John 13:(1–17) 18–20	25th Sunday in Ordinary Time
John 13:21–38	26th Sunday in Ordinary Time
John 15:18–25 (26–27); 16:1–4a	Trinity Sunday
John 16:16–24	2nd Sunday of Easter
John 16:25–33	3rd Sunday of Easter
John 18:1–12	28th Sunday in Ordinary Time
John 18:13–28	29th Sunday in Ordinary Time
John 18:29—19:16	30th Sunday in Ordinary Time
John 19:17–30	32nd Sunday in Ordinary Time
John 19:31–42	33rd Sunday in Ordinary Time
John 20:19–31	Resurrection Evening
John 21:20–25	Resurrection Evening
John 21:20–25	7th Sunday of Easter
Rom 1:8–15 (16–17) 18–32; 2:1–11	Sixth Sunday of Lent (Palm)
Rom 2:12–29	Maundy Thursday
Rom 3:1–22a	Christmas Morning (Proper II)
Rom 7:1–14	28th Sunday in Ordinary Time
Rom 9:6–33	29th Sunday in Ordinary Time
Rom 10:1–4, 16–21	30th Sunday in Ordinary Time
Rom 11:2b–28 (29–32) 33–36	Christmas Day (Proper III)
Rom 11:2b–28 (29–32) 33–36	30th Sunday in Ordinary Time
Rom 13:1–7; 14:13–23	32nd Sunday in Ordinary Time
Rom 15:1–3, 14–33	31st Sunday in Ordinary Time
Rom 16:1–25 (26–27)	33rd Sunday in Ordinary Time

1 Cor 3:12–15 (3:16—4:5) 4:6–21	13th Sunday in Ordinary Time
1 Cor 5:1–6a (6b–8) 9–13; 6:1–11	14th Sunday in Ordinary Time
1 Cor 7:1–40	15th Sunday in Ordinary Time
1 Cor 9:1–15 (16–18, 23)	16th Sunday in Ordinary Time
1 Cor 10:(14–17) 18—11:1	17th Sunday in Ordinary Time
1 Cor 11:2–22 (23–26) 27–34	19th Sunday in Ordinary Time
1 Cor 14:1–40	22nd Sunday in Ordinary Time
1 Cor 15:27–34 (35–38) 39–41 (42–58)	Holy Saturday (Great Vigil)
1 Cor 15:27–34 (35–38) 39–41 (42–58)	Christ the King
1 Cor 16:1–24	23rd Sunday in Ordinary Time
2 Cor 1:1–17 (18–22)	Resurrection of the LORD
2 Cor 1:23—2:17	2nd Sunday of Easter
2 Cor 3:7–11 (4:16—5:1) 5:2–5 (6–10)	Resurrection Evening
2 Cor 6:11—7:1	3rd Sunday of Easter
2 Cor 7:2–16	4th Sunday of Easter
2 Cor 8:1–6 (7–15) 16–24	5th Sunday of Easter
2 Cor 9:1–15	6th Sunday of Easter
2 Cor 10:1–17	7th Sunday of Easter
2 Cor 11:1—12:1	Pentecost Sunday
2 Cor 12:11–21; 13:1–10 (11–13)	Trinity Sunday
Gal (1:1–24)	Ash Wednesday
Gal (1:1–24)	First Sunday of Lent
Gal 2:1–14 (15–21)	First Sunday of Lent
Gal 2:1–14 (15–21)	Second Sunday of Lent
Gal 3:1–22 (23–29)	Third Sunday of Lent
Gal 4:1–3 (4–7) 8–31 (5:1)	Fourth Sunday of Lent
Gal 5:(1) 2–12 (13–25) 26	Fifth Sunday of Lent
Gal 6:1–6 (7–16) 17–18	Sixth Sunday of Lent (Palm)
Eph 2:11–22	Ash Wednesday
Eph 4:17–24 (26–32; 5:1–2) 3–7	11th Sunday in Ordinary Time

Eph 5:21–33; 6:1–9 (10–20) 21–24	26th Sunday in Ordinary Time
Phil 1:1–2 (3–11) 12–20	Resurrection of the LORD
Phil 2:14–30	9th Sunday in Ordinary Time
Phil 3:1–4a; 4:10–23	Christmas Eve (Proper I)
Phil 3:1–4a; 4:10–23	33rd Sunday in Ordinary Time
Col 1:29—2:5 (16–19) 20–23	21st Sunday in Ordinary Time
Col 3:18—4:18	27th Ordinary (World Communion)
1 Tim 3:1–16	20th Sunday in Ordinary Time
1 Tim 4:1–16	12th Sunday in Ordinary Time
1 Tim 5:1–23	24th Sunday in Ordinary Time
Titus 1:1–16	25th Sunday in Ordinary Time
Heb 1:13—2:4	First Sunday of Advent
Heb 3:1–19	Second Sunday of Advent
Heb 4:1–11 (12–16)	Third Sunday of Advent
Heb 5:11—6:20	Fourth Sunday of Advent
Heb 7:1–28	First Sunday of Christmas
Heb 8:1–13	Second Sunday of Christmas
Heb 9:1–28	Baptism of the LORD (First Ordinary)
Heb 10:1–4 (10–14) 26–39	Second Sunday in Ordinary Time
Heb 11:(1–3) 4–7, 17–28 (39–40)	Third Sunday in Ordinary Time
Heb 12:(1–3) 4–17	Fourth Sunday in Ordinary Time
Heb 13:9–14 (15–16) 17–25	Fifth Sunday in Ordinary Time
Heb 13:9–14, 17–25	Transfiguration Sunday
Jas 1:1–16 (17–27)	First Sunday of Lent
Jas 1:1–16	Ash Wednesday
Jas (1:17–27)	Christmas Eve (Proper I)
Jas (1:17—2:10) 2:11–13	First Sunday of Lent

Jas (2:1–10) 11–13 (14–17) 18–26	Second Sunday of Lent
Jas 2:(14–17) 18–26	Second Sunday of Lent
Jas (3:1–18)	Third Sunday of Lent
Jas 4:(1–3) 4–6 (7–8a) 8b–17	Fourth Sunday of Lent
Jas 5:1–6 (7–10) 11–12 (13–20)	Fifth Sunday of Lent
1 Pet 2:1, 11–18 (19–25); 3:1–12	27th Sunday of Ordinary Time
1 Pet 4:(1–8) 9–11 (12–14) 15–19	Good Friday
2 Pet 1:1–15	Sixth Sunday in Ordinary Time
2 Pet 2:1–22	Seventh Sunday in Ordinary Time
2 Pet 2:1–22	11th Sunday in Ordinary Time
2 Pet 2:1–22	18th Sunday in Ordinary Time
2 Pet 3:1–7 (8–14) 15–18	Eighth Sunday in Ordinary Time
1 John 2:3–29	Epiphany (January 6)
1 John 2:3–29	Ascension (Thursday)
1 John 2:3–29	18th Sunday in Ordinary Time
1 John 3:8–15 (16–24); 4:1–6	10th Sunday in Ordinary Time
2 John 1–13	13th Sunday in Ordinary Time
2 John 1–13	18th Sunday in Ordinary Time
3 John 1–15	All Saints' Day
Jude 1–25	Transfiguration Sunday
Rev 1:1–3 (4–8) 9–20	Resurrection Evening

Appendix C
Scheduling Options

SINCE THE TEXT SELECTIONS FOR YEAR D ARE OFTEN LENGTHIER THAN those in the *RCL*, this may, in many cases, require additional refinement and narrowing in the selections, based on liturgical and pastoral considerations, time constraints, and other concerns, and it will inevitably add significant variety. Many Year D texts are less familiar; some are extraordinarily difficult and some just plain bewildering. Thus, the very design of Year D (with longer lections and fewer ready-made resources) will likely entail more time in the study—hint: that is a *good* thing!—if the worship service is to have focus, coherence, and not overtax the physical stamina of the congregation. It may be wise to invest in some advance planning, study, and prayer before embarking on Year D, and to do so in consultation with staff, colleagues, and others who may be willing and able to work on developing more liturgical resources than are currently available.

On the other hand, studying Year D alongside other weekly exegetical, preaching, and liturgical duties may divide one's focus and defer the application of much needed nourishment. In this case, it is probably better to plunge right in, for the church today desperately needs these texts, far more desperately than pastors can afford the luxury of lingering over the decision. The texts that comprise Year D will make their own case for lectionary expansion, for once one begins to search them, one finds oneself saying, as I have said again and again, "How can it be that *that* text is not in the lectionary?"

Meanwhile, let us consider the scheduling options more programmatically. A quadrennial supplement to a three-year lectionary cycle presents some complications, but they are not insurmountable. As mentioned in chapter 1, the effect of many churches using Year D when many other churches do not will likely set up a cross-rhythm, a sequence of inter-weaving three-year and four-year cycles. Comparing Option X to the *RCL* in the table (below), one can see how the cross-rhythm pattern by which, after three cycles of four years and four cycles of three years, everything will "come 'round right."

Option Y, on the other hand, adapts the three-year cycle by integrating Year D into the rotation by means of regular alternating substitutions for Years A, B, and C, each in turn. Option Y thus maintains the same three-year rhythm as the *RCL*—moving in waltz time, so to speak—but alters the standard *RCL* pattern every fourth year.

Both X and Y strike a good balance with the *RCL*, and while this may be desirable in the long run, the fact is that Year D is intended to correct a situation that is currently imbalanced and unstable. Hence, to use the nutritional metaphor, as one discovers in Year D the rich scriptural nutrients that have been missing in the church's diet, one may be inclined to accelerate the use of Year D in the near term on an *ad hoc* basis, perhaps by focusing on different parts of the canon OR different options (for there are a number of them). Thus, Option Z could take a number of different possible modes: an annual substitution (Z1), season by season (Z2), Sunday by Sunday (Z3), OR using a Sunday-by-Sunday hybrid (Z4).

An annual substitution (Z1) would simply mean plugging Year D into any year when the pastor thinks the variation would be helpful OR necessary. One could simply return to the *RCL* after that and pick up where one left off (one year behind the *RCL*), OR in sync with the *RCL* cycle itself. (The table below offers an example of one such option.)

Another option is to try Year D for a season—Advent OR Lent OR Easter, OR the Passion—thus exercising Option Z2. This may be best for pastors OR churches for whom a particular season has become stagnant and routine, where a longer commitment is simply out of reach for the time being, OR where a particular emphasis presented in Year D is warranted (e.g., the apocalyptic discourse, OR the Passion).

For those who do not preach frequently, Option Z3 may be attractive. After consulting the scheduled selections per the *RCL*, one might compare Year D to consider some alternative readings from different perspectives within the canon. This can open up some unforeseen dimensions.

A further variation on this theme is a hybrid option. Permit me to illustrate anecdotally. On a recent Transfiguration Sunday, some fresh insights emerged into the familiar *RCL* gospel lection by juxtaposing it with a variety of Year D lections (Psalm, OT, and Epistle), not all of them from Transfiguration Sunday itself, but from various parts of the "Index of Lections." In short, by retaining the *RCL* gospel lection and varying the other lections drawn from Year D, a hybrid option (Z4) emerged. Happily, the result was a stronger than usual Transfiguration sermon.

Such "diversity" is not necessarily "divisive" and may in fact be very fruitful and creative. Certainly, we would do well to remember the considerable freedom, flexibility, and discretion that ministers in the Reformed tradition (and beyond) have in text selection—a point that even the designers of the *RCL* insist is how the three-year instrument is to be used. With this in mind, we should certainly question the simplistic notion that ecclesial unity is necessarily enhanced by conformity to the lectionary. Indeed, we may well have discovered grounds for concluding that a *reductive* lectionary actually does more to exacerbate ecclesial *dis*unity than it does to unify the church. Perhaps the ecumenical church's most creative response to such a state of affairs is, yes, to expand the lectionary, and in the interim, to consider the textual departures from a three-year cycle no more threatening than polyphony is in relation to the "unity" of monophonic plainsong (unless it wanders off into a completely arhythmic spasm). In other words, adding a plurality of scriptural voices to the church year promises to add what new musical "parts" add to melody: complexity and (I dare say) even "glory." But on that score, as on every other, we must reserve judgment for God.

Year	*RCL*	X (4-year) [Cross-rhythm]	Y (3-year) [Adapted *RCL*]	Z (1) [*Ad hoc*]
2011–12	B	B	B	B
2012–13	C	C	D (in lieu of C)	D (Gospels)
2013–14	A	D	A	A
2014–15	B	A	B	D (Epistles)
2015–16	C	B	C	C
2016–17	A	C	D (in lieu of A)	D (OT)
2017–18	B	D	B	B
2018–19	C	A	C	D (Pss)
2019–20	A	B	A	A
2020–21	B	C	D (in lieu of B)	D (Gospels)

2021–22	C	D	C	C
2022–23	A	A	A	**D** (Epistles)
2023–24	B	B	B	B
2024–25	C	C	**D** (in lieu of C)	C
2025–26	A	**D**	A	A
2026–27	B	A	B	**D** (OT)
2027–28	C	B	C	C
2028–29	A	C	**D** (in lieu of A)	A
2029–30	B	**D**	B	B
2030–31	C	A	C	**D** (Psalms)
2031–32	A	B	A	A
2032–33	B	C	**D** (in lieu of B)	B
2033–34	C	**D**	C	C
2034–35	A	A	A	**D** (Gospels)

Bibliography

Aland, Kurt, editor. *Synopsis of the Four Gospels*. 8th corrected ed. Stuttgart: German Bible Society, 1987.

Allen, Horace T., Jr. "Introduction: Preaching in a Christian Context." In *Handbook for the Revised Common Lectionary*, edited by Peter C. Bower, 1–24. Louisville: Westminster John Knox, 1996.

———. "Using the Consensus Lectionary." In *Social Themes of the Christian Year: A Commentary on the Lectionary*, edited by Dieter T. Hessel, 264–68. Philadelphia: Geneva, 1983.

Allen, Ronald J. *Interpreting the Gospel: An Introduction to Preaching*. St. Louis: Chalice, 1998.

Allmen, Jean-Jacques von. *Preaching and Congregation*. Richmond: John Knox, 1962.

———. *Worship: Its Theology and Practice*. Oxford: Oxford University Press, 1965.

Anderson, Bernard W. *Out of the Depths: The Psalms Speak for Us Today*. Revised and Expanded Edition. Philadelphia: The Westminster Press, 1983.

Aulén, Gustav. *Christus Victor: An Historical Study of the Three Main Types of the Idea of the Atonement*. Translated by A. G. Hebert. New York: Macmillan, 1958.

Barth, Karl. *Call for God*. Translated by A. T. Mackay. New York: Harper & Row, 1967.

———. *CD. 1/1: The Doctrine of the Word of God*. Edited and translated by G. W. Bromiley and T. F. Torrance. 2nd ed. Edinburgh: T. & T. Clark, 1975.

———. *Deliverance to the Captives*. Translated by Marguerite Wieser. New York: Harper, 1961.

———. *Homiletics*. Translated by G. W. Bromiley and D. E. Daniels. Louisville: Westminster John Knox, 1991.

———. *Prayer*. 50th anniversary ed. Edited by Don E. Saliers. Translated by Sara F. Terrien. Louisville: Westminster John Knox, 2002.

———. *The Word of God and the Word of Man*. Translated by Douglas Horton. Gloucester, MA: Peter Smith, 1978.

Bartow, Charles L. *God's Human Speech: A Practical Theology of Proclamation*. Grand Rapids: Eerdmans, 1997.

Berkhof, Louis. *Systematic Theology*. Edinburgh: The Banner of Truth Trust, 1958.

Bonhoeffer, Dietrich. *Discipleship*. Edited by Geffrey B. Kelly and John D. Godsey. Translated by Barbara Green and Reinhard Krauss. *Dietrich Bonhoeffer Works 4*. Minneapolis: Fortress, 2001.

Bower, Peter C. "Introduction." In *Handbook for the Common Lectionary*, edited by Peter C. Bower, 15–40. Philadelphia: Geneva, 1987.

Brueggemann, Walter. *The Book That Breathes New Life: Scriptural Authority and Biblical Theology*. Minneapolis: Fortress, 2005.

———. *The Message of the Psalms*. Minneapolis: Augsburg, 1984.

———. *The Word Militant: Preaching a Decentering Word*. Minneapolis: Fortress, 2010.

Cherry, Constance M. *The Worship Architect: A Blueprint for Designing Culturally Relevant and Biblically Faithful Services*. Grand Rapids: Baker Academic, 2010.

The Consultation on Common Texts. *The Revised Common Lectionary*. Nashville: Abingdon, 1992.

Craddock, Fred. *As One Without Authority*. 3rd ed. Nashville: Abingdon, 1979.

Dawn, Marva J. *How Shall We Worship? Biblical Guidelines for the Worship Wars*. Carol Stream, IL: Tyndale House, 2003.

———. *Reaching Out without Dumbing Down: A Theology of Worship for This Urgent Time*. Grand Rapids: Eerdmans, 1995.

Day, John N. *Crying for Justice: What the Psalms Teach Us about Mercy and Vengeance in an Age of Terrorism*. Grand Rapids: Kregel, 2005.

De Arteaga, William L. *Forgotten Power: The Significance of the Lord's Supper in Revival*. Grand Rapids: Zondervan, 2002.

Dozeman, Thomas B. "Canonical Criticism." In *The New Interpreter's Handbook of Preaching*, edited by Paul Scott Wilson et al., 15–17. Nashville: Abingdon, 2008.

Duba, Arlo D. "'Righteous Judgment' and Biblical Preaching." *PO*, 22 March 2004, 8–9, 20.

———. "Righteous Judgment: What Does the Congregation Hear?" *PO*, 8 November 2004, 11–13, 17.

Exum, J. Cheryl. *Fragmented Women*. Sheffield, UK: Sheffield Academic Press, 1993.

Fant, Clyde E. *Bonhoeffer: Worldly Preaching*. Nashville: Thomas Nelson, 1975.

Farrar, Frederic William. *Mercy and Judgment: A Few Last Words on Christian Eschatology*. New York: Dutton, 1881.

Forde, Gerhard O. *Theology Is for Proclamation*. Minneapolis: Fortress, 1990.

Forsyth, Peter Taylor. *Positive Preaching and Modern Mind*. Carlisle, Cumbria, UK: Paternoster, 1998.

Fuller, Reginald H. "Lectionary." In *The New Westminster Dictionary of Liturgy and Worship*, edited by J. G. Davies, 297–99. Philadelphia: Westminster, 1986.

Goldingay, John. "Canon and Lection." In *To Glorify God: Essays on Modern Reformed Liturgy*, edited by Bryan D. Spinks and Iain R. Torrance, 85–97. Grand Rapids: Eerdmans, 1999.

Goodloe, IV, James C. "Duba Overstates Benign Influence of Lectionary." *PO*, 21 June 2004, 7, 11, 14.

———. "Righteous Judgment." *PO*, 5 January 2004, 12–13.

Holladay, William L. *The Psalms through Three Thousand Years: Prayerbook of a Cloud of Witnesses*. Minneapolis: Fortress, 1996.

Joint Liturgical Group (JLG 2). *A Four Year Lectionary*. Norwich, UK: Canterbury, 1990.

Kay, James F. *Christus Præsens: A Reconsideration of Rudolf Bultmann's Christology*. Grand Rapids: Eerdmans, 1994.

Kahler, Martin. *The So-Called Historical Jesus and the Historic Biblical Christ*. Translated by Carl E. Braaten. Philadelphia: Fortress, 1964.

Kelsey, David H. *The Uses of Scripture in Recent Theology*. Philadelphia: Fortress, 1975.

Kierkegaard, Søren. *Christian Discourses; The Crisis and a Crisis in the Life of an Actress.* Edited and translated by Howard V. Hong and Edna H. Hong. Kierkegaard's Writings 17. Princeton, NJ: Princeton University Press, 1997.

———. *For Self-Examination; Judge for Yourself!* Edited and translated by Howard V. Hong and Edna H. Hong. Kierkegaard's Writings 21. Princeton, NJ: Princeton University Press, 1990.

———. *The Moment and Late Writings.* Edited and translated by Howard V. Hong and Edna H. Hong. Kierkegaard's Writings 23. Princeton, NJ: Princeton University Press, 1998.

———. *Practice in Christianity.* Edited and translated by Howard V. Hong and Edna H. Hong. Kierkegaard's Writings 20. Princeton, NJ: Princeton University Press, 1991.

Lischer, Richard. *A Theology of Preaching: The Dynamics of the Gospel.* Rev. ed. Eugene, OR: Wipf and Stock, 2001.

Long, Thomas G. *Beyond the Worship Wars: Building Vital and Faithful Worship.* Bethesda, MD: Alban Institute, 2001.

———. *The Witness of Preaching.* 2nd ed. Louisville: Westminster John Knox, 2005.

Lose, David J. *Confessing Jesus Christ: Preaching in a Postmodern World.* Grand Rapids: Eerdmans, 2003.

Lowry, Eugene. *Living with the Lectionary.* Nashville: Abingdon, 1992.

Luther, Martin. *Ninety-five Theses.* In *Martin Luther: Selections from His Writings,* edited by John Dillenberger, 489–500. Garden City, NY: Doubleday, 1961.

Maxwell, William D. *An Outline of Christian Worship: Its Development and Forms.* London: Oxford University Press, 1960.

McCarthur, A. Allan. *The Christian Year and Lectionary Reform.* London: SCM, 1958.

———. *The Evolution of the Christian Year.* Greenwich, CT: Seabury, 1953.

Meuser, Fred W. *Luther the Preacher.* Minneapolis: Augsburg, 1983.

Nestle, Eberhard, and Kurt Aland. *Novum Testamentum Graece.* 26th ed. Stuttgart: Deutsche Bibelstiftung, 1979.

Old, Hughes Oliphant. "*Lectio Continua* and the Lectionary." *PO,* 21 June 2004, 6, 12.

———. *The Patristic Roots of Reformed Worship.* Zürich: Theologischer Verlag, 1975.

———. *The Reading and Preaching of the Scriptures in the Worship of the Christian Church.* 7 vols. Grand Rapids: Eerdmans, 1998–2010.

———. *Worship: That Is Reformed according to Scripture.* Atlanta: John Knox, 1984.

Phelps, Austin. *Theory of Preaching: Lectures on Homiletics.* New York: Scribners, 1881.

Rupprecht, Johannes. *Hermann Bezzel als Theologe.* München: Chr. Kaiser, 1925.

Rutledge, Fleming. *Not Ashamed of the Gospel.* Grand Rapids: Eerdmans, 2007.

Saliers, Donald E. *Worship and Spirituality.* 2nd ed. Memphis: OSL, 1996.

Sanders, James A. "Canon and Calendar." In *Social Themes of the Christian Year: A Commentary on the Lectionary,* edited by Dieter T. Hessel, 257–63. Philadelphia: Geneva, 1983.

Slemmons, Timothy Matthew. "Expand the Lectionary! The Need for and Features of Supplementary Year D." *The Academy of Homiletics: Papers of the Annual Meeting, 42nd Mtg.* Minneapolis/St. Paul: Academy of Homiletics, 2007.

———. *Groans of the Spirit: Homiletical Dialectics in an Age of Confusion.* Eugene, OR: Pickwick, 2010.

———. "*Synkrinesis* as Following in Faith: Interpretation for a Kerygmatic Homiletic." In *KOINONIA* 13:2 (2001) 347–59.

———. "Toward a Penitential Homiletic: Authority and Direct Communication in Christian Proclamation." PhD diss., Princeton Theological Seminary, 2004.

Spinks, Bryan D. "Christian Worship or Cultural Incantations?" *Studia Liturgia* 12 (1977) 1–19.

Stookey, Laurence Hull. *Calendar: Christ's Time for the Church.* Nashville: Abingdon, 1996.

———. "Lectionary and the Christian Year." In *The New Interpreter's Handbook of Preaching*, edited by Paul Scott Wilson et al., 321–25. Nashville: Abingdon, 2008.

Stott, John. *Between Two Worlds: The Challenge of Preaching Today.* Grand Rapids: Eerdmans, 1982.

Talley, Thomas J. *The Origins of the Liturgical Year.* New York: Pueblo, 1986.

Thompson, Bard. *Liturgies of the Western Church.* Reprint, Philadelphia: Fortress, 1980.

Trotter, J. Irwin. "Are We Preaching a Subversive Lectionary?" *School of Theology at Claremont Bulletin: Occasional Paper Number 7*, 28:2 (1985) 1–2.

Van Ens, Jack. "Fearful Preachers Don't Fire at the War Elephant." *PO*, 4 September 2006. Online: http://www.pres-outlook.com/opinion3/guest-commentary3/2782.html.

Vatican Council II. "Constitution on the Liturgy," *Sacrosantum Concilium* (4 December 1963). Translated by the International Committee on English in the Liturgy. In *Documents on the Liturgy, 1963–1979: Conciliar, Papal, and Curial Texts.* Collegeville, MN: Liturgical, 1982.

Wainwright, Geoffrey. *Doxology: In Praise of God in Worship, Doctrine, and Life: A Systematic Theology.* New York: Oxford University Press, 1980.

Webber, Robert E. *Ancient-Future Faith: Rethinking Evangelicalism for a Postmodern World.* Grand Rapids: Baker, 1999.

———. *Ancient-Future Time: Forming Spirituality through the Christian Year.* Grand Rapids: Baker, 2004.

———. *Ancient-Future Worship: Proclaiming and Enacting God's Narrative.* Grand Rapids: Baker, 2008.

Westerfield Tucker, Karen B. "Lectionary Preaching." In *Concise Encyclopedia of Preaching*, edited by William H. Willimon and Richard Lischer, 305–7. Louisville: Westminster John Knox, 1995.

White, James F. *A Brief History of Christian Worship.* Nashville: Abingdon, 1993.

———. *Introduction to Christian Worship.* 3rd ed. Nashville: Abingdon, 2000.

Willimon, William H., and Richard Lischer, editors. *Concise Encyclopedia of Preaching.* Louisville: Westminster John Knox, 1995.

Wilson, Paul Scott. *Imagination of the Heart.* Nashville: Abingdon, 1988.